THE PSYCHIC
Dolphins, DNA & the Planetary Grid

Hugh Newman

This book is dedicated to the soul that visited Emma & myself in March 2007. With blessings and farewell from Lundy Island, we await your return...

Acknowledgements

Thank you to all the Indigo children who have inspired & influenced this book. A big thank you to my mother – Meg Newman, Emma Stoner, Jake Ewen, Ben Cummins for being my true brother, Sian Newman, Megan & Melissa Casey, Gill Newman, Shaun Casey, Emmanuel Martin, Jules Salt, John Martineau, Michael Glickman, Geoff Stray for proofing and revelations, Stuart Mason, Michael Hanby, Saqqara Price, Saleena Ki, Crystal Skull Vicky, Simon Peter Fuller, John Michell, Gareth Mills, Shaun 'Geo-Repair Man' Kirwan, David Hatfield – the Gnaughty Gnome, Susan Malleson, Nigel Blair (RIP), Suzi Steer, Mark Poyner, Karen Smith, Simon Penton, Edmund Marriage, Tor Webster, Nandan O'Leary, Giles Bryant, James Twyman, Ashearon Hobson, Dan Winter, Louis Standen, Paradox, Carl Murphy, Mark Heley, Tim Learmount, Rita Hraiz & everyone else who has inspired, educated and supported the eventual publication of this book.

Cover Design

Front cover artwork 'Begin' by Seraiel Grace-Mantle, who I met in Hawaii at the 'Psychic Children speak to the World' conference. www.breath-of-grace.com.

General cover design and logo artwork by Carl 'Youri' Sullivan. www.juicyworlds.com.

Copyright

No part of this book may be used or reproduced in any form without permission from the author except in the case of quotations, articles and reviews. Images and diagrams in this book have been carefully chosen and attempts have been made to obtain permission from the relevant authors and publishers. If anyone has any queries, I am pleased to make suitable arrangements to copyright holders whom it has not been possible to contact so that any future editions may be amended and sources acknowledged. Please contact the author: hugh@psychicchildren.co.uk

Glastonbury, UK
ISBN: 978-0956786500

Copyright © 2005-2007 Hugh Newman – www.psychicchildren.co.uk

CONTENTS

INTRODUCTION

1. **THE CHILDREN – page 7**
   Babysitting psychic children / The Indigo children / China's super-psychics / Children of the Blue-Ray / Crystal children / Prophecies.

2. **THE HAWAII CONFERENCE – page 14**
   The Mexico initiation / Grandma Chandra / The 'Lemuria' ceremony / The conference begins / The star tetrahedron / Stargates / Lizzie / Zach / Koya / The dolphins & the whales / Thomas & the crop circle / Sonar experiments / Underwater UFOs

3. **THE PLANETARY GRID – page 32**
   The Platonic solids / Icosahedron grid / The great pyramid / Icosa-dodecahedron grid / Metatron and angels / Working with the grid / The human effect

4. **NUTRITION FOR THE NEW HUMAN – page 48**
   Alternatives to ritalin / Avoidance tactics / Hydrogenated fats / Exciototoxins / Sugar blues / Sugar alternatives / Pesticides / Something in the water / Babycare products / Pregnancy / Water birthing / Vaccination dangers / Nutritional recommendations / Essential fats / Natural nutrition / Vitamins and minerals / Beneficial bacteria / Etherium gold / Mobile phones and masts

5. **DNA ATIVATION – page 73**
   The forgotten codes / Blood types and DNA / Ancient genetics / ORME's and M-state elements / Russian junk DNA research / The cosmic serpent

6. **GALACTIC ALIGNMENT 2012 – page 86**
   DNA and solar radiation / The heliosphere / The photon belt / Galactic superwave / galactic alignment / the octahedral universe

7. **BREATHING IN THE COSMOS – page 96**

   Appendix: Planetary Grid Points – page 99
   References – page 101

An inspirational painting of Grandmother Chandra by my good friend Rob, who created this without ever meeting Chandra. I had just got back from Hawaii after meeting her & then met Rob at a festival in the UK where I was speaking about my research. He presented this to me, and to our astonishment it beautifully resembled her. Thank you Rob.

INTRODUCTION

There is an increasing awareness of the 'new' children that are currently incarnating on earth. The many books about 'Indigo' and 'Crystal' children are slowly leaking in to our consciousness. The stories of powerful psychic and telepathic abilities amaze us and the angelic words they utter melt our hearts. The Psychic children are well and truly here.

As these children become more accepted in society, many questions are still not being answered. Why are they incarnating now? What is their purpose? Why do some of them have incredible psychic abilities? What does it mean to humanity? And ultimately what can we do to facilitate this amazing natural process of human transformation? Some of the children can clearly remember past lives. Some communicate from their mother's womb. The stories keep coming in and now we are starting to get some answers.

There are several core topics that have been opened up which are helping unlock the secrets of the Psychic children. It is now evident that our DNA is rapidly mutating and the children are the first to show the signs. The alignment of our solar system with galactic centre in 2012 is also intimately connected. This book also investigates the earth's energy grid and delves into how it is being repaired by the children and fellow light workers and explores the astonishing grid-work the dolphins and the whales are undertaking in the oceans. The children and the dolphins are resonating with each other, and rather than question what is happening (like adults), the kids get on with it.

Through this research, cutting edge information has been revealed that is now being opened up to the public domain. It was not long ago that this type of information was only in the hands of high-level initiates of various Masonic lodges. But thanks to the children, the Internet and our evolving consciousness, the information is being revealed at a rate faster than ever before. We are at a point in history where the other dimensions are only a breath away. The veil is so thin now that we all can journey through just by being pure of heart and in the present moment. The kids teach that love is the key to everywhere and everything, and soon we will see that it is they who are now leading the way into the next dimension.

Authors Note: Although this book appeared in earlier incarnations during 2004 and 2005, it has now had an update to align it with new discoveries and revelations about the current shift in consciousness that is taking place and the role the Psychic children are playing in this process.

Hugh Newman

*The children with the second sight
a natural thing so that they might
grow graceful, humble and when they do
the Golden Age will start anew*

*The Prophecy of Mother Shipton
circa 1530AD*

1. THE CHILDREN

There was a short chapter in Drunvalo Melchizedek's *The Ancient Secret of the Flower of Life*, that opened my mind to the realm of the Psychic children. This eye-opening book stimulated something within me that has lasted to this day, but it was the information about these children that would just not let go. I began researching Drunvalo's claims and uncovered certain information that led to an article for a London based underground magazine (*Shangri-la-la*). Even before I submitted the piece in early 1999, I unconsciously opened up a new page on my computer and wrote *"Chapter 2……"*. Why I did this, I was not sure. It wasn't until a few months later that the answer was unveiled.

Two children came into my life who were born three years apart and after spending long periods of time with them both, I realised that they were part of the unfolding journey that is this book. Ki, a five year old (at the time), gave me my first experience of an Indigo child. He was an incredible being. I have never seen such a warrior at such a young age. His passion was war games, chess, fighting, swordplay and anything competitive. Babysitting Ki was a challenge. His Mother had warned me about his behaviour, but I felt connected to him, so I agreed to the job.

It became quite stressful looking after Ki, but this gave me an insight into what parents of Indigo children have to deal with. He was aggressive, impatient, demanding, loud and generally obnoxious. But at the same time, he showed deep compassion, an understanding of complex concepts and was alarmingly intelligent. I got many future glimpses of Ki. I often saw him as a military officer, or as the leader of the revolution. This child was an accomplished chess player by the time I met him and did not like to lose. In fact, he would do anything to win.

The traits I have mentioned are several 'classic' examples of an Indigo child, but to this day, I have felt something different with Ki. I believe he will step into his role as a leader and with such traits (or advantages) at such a young age; he is destined to become a 'John Connor', or a leader of the revolution. He also showed glimpses of psychic ability by correctly answering questions before his Mother had fully said them.

Before we go on, we must address the nature of labelling our children with terms such as 'Indigo' or 'Crystal'. Labels and categories such as these are being applied to these kids, but to say that one child is more 'special' than another, defeats the object of opening up this phenomenon to the general public. It can also give the child's ego something to feed on. Labels such as 'ADD' and 'ADHD' are already under scrutiny, but to label kids with 'Crystal' or 'Indigo' can put them on a pedestal and could possibly lead to problems in the future. During this book I use these labels loosely, but to establish a coherent understanding of the process of accelerated evolution over the last twenty-five years, I have followed on from previous authors by continuing to use terms such as 'Indigo' or 'Crystal'. Ultimately there are no labels, just a period of human development and a quickening in the expansion of consciousness. Gary Zukav sums it up In his book, *Soul Stories*. "*'Give me the best flower that you have', said a man to a florist. 'Every flower here is the best', replied the florist. At these words, the man became enlightened"*.

Like Ki, the Indigo children have a warrior nature, a 'rebel with a cause' personality with absolutely no guilt. They are often labelled as hyperactive or aggressive, but this is their purpose. They are here to break down old and outmoded systems – legal, educational, medical, you name it, these kids are here to force honesty and integrity on a global level. Telepathy and other psychic abilities are rife amongst the Indigos, who are leading us into a telepathic society; a society that must be based on the Indigo principles for it to function effectively. Telepathy cannot work if dishonesty and deceit are present. We must remember that Indigos have been incarnating for about twenty-five years now, so it won't be long before they get into positions of power to enable the changes they are destined for. They are natural leaders, hacking away the old and leaving an open path for the new children.

During the late seventies, Nancy Ann Tappe; a pioneer in the study of 'life colours' noticed changes taking place in the colour of children's auras. She taught at the University of San Diego and as part of her research she published a book in 1982 called *Understanding Your Life Through Color*. This is where the first mention of 'Indigo' is written about. Lee Carol and Jan Tober, authors of *The Indigo Children* and *Indigo Celebration* published Tappe's research on varying colours of the aura. Tappe describes the life colour as, "*the single color of the aura that remains constant in most people from the cradle to the grave.... The life color establishes a focus for the entire lifetime, similar to having a major in college*". Tappe recognized that after 1980 about 80% of the babies being born had this aura around them that she equated to their life mission and their life colour. It was what she called Indigo. As of 1990 she realized that the Indigo birth rate had risen to about 90%.

"The Indigo phenomenon has been recognized as one of the most exciting changes in human nature ever documented in society. The Indigo label describes the energy pattern of human behaviour which exists in over 95% of the children born in the last 10 years... This phenomenon is happening globally and eventually the Indigos will replace all other colors. As small children, Indigos are easy to recognize by their unusually large, clear eyes. Extremely bright, precocious children with an amazing memory and a strong desire to live instinctively, these children of the next millennium are sensitive, gifted souls with an evolved consciousness who have come here to help change the vibrations of our lives and create one land, one globe and one species. They are our bridge to the future".

Indigo is the colour of the third eye chakra, which is an energy centre inside the head located between the two eyebrows. This chakra regulates clairvoyance, or the ability to see energy, visions and spirits, so many of the Indigo children are often classed as clairvoyant. Nancy was able to carry out this unique research because she has a medical diagnosis of Synesthesia. That's where two neurological pathways become crossed so that the senses get reversed. She actually sees like a Kirlian camera. What seems to be her dysfunction has ended up being a great gift.

The Indigos are frequently misdiagnosed with Attention Deficit Disorder (ADD), Attention Deficit Hyperactivity Disorder (ADHD) and more recently Oppositional Defiant Disorder (ODD) [1]. This is because of their warrior nature. Parents can't handle this intense energy and often think the only way to calm them down is to numb them with powerful pharmaceutical psycho-stimulants. Ritalin is an example of such a drug that has been known to cause severe side effects that have lasted for years. Teachers in America even recommend that parents give Ritalin to the children! According to Nancy Ann Tappe, these children have right and left-brain coherence, something people on the spiritual path strive for throughout their lifetime. They are also very sensitive, have psychic abilities and possess incredible wisdom, as though they are old souls in young bodies. Evidence for the reincarnation process is becoming a reality as more and more of these children remember their past lives. Some remember all of their past lives as we shall see later.

Drunvalo Melchizedek, who was an early investigator of the Indigo children, heard many reports from parents about the incredible intelligence of these kids. (Ki is no exception; he could win at chess at four years old). It seems that schools cannot contain this innate quality and therefore label them with these disorders. But some of these children have extremely high IQ's. Some at genius level of 160, and many at around 130. It's not that their attention is distracted or they can't concentrate, it's more to do with the fact that they process information very quickly and understand things intuitively, which leads to extreme boredom in these kids' minds. Basically they get frustrated with outdated and outmoded teaching methods and therefore 'play up' to the teachers. Nancy Ann Tappe says, "*Indigos are like 220 volts placed into 110 wiring.*" We can't contain these children in these environments any more. It's not the kids who have to change, it's the system that has to, and fortunately this is becoming more and more recognised by certain governments around the world. The Indigo child phenomenon is not restricted to one area. Similar qualities have been noted all over the planet.

The 'Super Psychics' of China, have been recognised and nurtured by their government for the last twenty-five years. Corresponding to the time frame of the Indigos, and recognised by Nancy Ann Tappe in her early research, the phenomenon in China has reached a critical point. Paul Dong and Thomas E. Raffill, authors of *China's Super Psychics* state that millions of dollars have been spent researching EHF, or 'Extra Human Functions' in these children. Schools and research centres are widespread throughout the country. By 1997, 100,000 of these children had been recognised

One skill the children were able to develop was 'psychic writing', a technique where they were asked to imagine some written words on a blank piece of paper inside a pencil case. The case would be closed, then a short time later reopened, and on it were the words written in pencil. A girl from Shanghai called Xiao Kiong was the first to demonstrate this ability and so in 1981, EHF researchers at Yunnan Wenshan Teachers' College in Yunna Province selected five children with EHF for further training. It was soon found that when blindfolded, these children were able to see with their ears, nose, mouth, tongue, armpits, hands or feet. The tests were flawless. American new-age magazine Omni got involved when the tests were set up to check there could be no cheating.

Another example was when a page was ripped from a random book and placed in the armpit of one of the children. The child could read every single word on the page perfectly in the right order. After many more tests Omni magazine became convinced these kids were for real. But Omni were not the only ones present. Zhu Yiyi, editor of Shanghai's Nature Magazine, a prestigious science journal, also witnessed these events. On another occasion, a thousand people were sitting in an auditorium and were each given a rosebud. A six-year-old girl came on stage and with a silent wave of her hand; the rosebuds would slowly open to fully blossom into beautiful roses before the eyes of the astonished audience.

Another child would take a sealed bottle off a shelf at random and place it at the centre of a table. After a few moments the pills passed through the glass bottle and settled on the table. In many cases, the child would then take another object, such as a coin, put it on the table and it would levitate into the sealed bottle. Is this showing signs of higher-dimensional consciousness?

Getting back to the story, the other child I connected with was Orion (or Onion as I like to call him). Orion is at the other end of the spectrum from Indigos. He is almost a polar opposite of Ki. Orion is 'labelled' a Blue-Ray or Crystal child. He is quiet and often listens in to conversations without anyone noticing. He is very intelligent and seems to float about the place when he is at home. He has a light and soft way about him. He is becoming an accomplished healer, thanks to his Mother; and he is very good at it. Reiki is his favoured mode. Deep, spiritual insights often fall out of his mouth, without him even realising what he has said. He is also very cheeky and manipulates the situation to get what he wants.

Gordon Michael Scallion first mentioned The 'Blue-Ray' children in the 1988 book *Notes From The Cosmos*. Scallion is an established psychic and modern-day prophet, often compared to Nostradamus and Edgar Cayce. He is probably most famous for his 'future maps' of the world and his predictions of earth changes. He was popularised in Bob Frissell's books, *Nothing in this Book is True* and *Something in this Book is True*. Scallion has known about these children since the early eighties, but did not really know what the significance was. It wasn't until 1988 that during a session with a client he went into trance and the information came out. He described the Blue-ray children as the forerunners of the new root race, who were from the 'mental' plane of existence, whose colour vibration was 'blue'. He explained that they were the souls from the ancient land of Lemuria, whereas the Indigos are predominantly Atlantean. According to Scallion, the Indigos laid the groundwork for the Blue-rays, which enabled them step into their roles as teachers. The indigo and blue colours are very close in the colour spectrum and this can be seen as a natural process of movement through subtle vibrations.

Scallion emphasised that these children 'evolve' very quickly "*They are teaching others by the age of four or five. By the time they reach their twelfth year, the Blue Ones would be equivalent to an average adult who has spent perhaps twenty-five years as a teacher*". They also have telekinetic powers, a 'knowing' of their mission on earth and many traits associated with all the other categories of children. Here is a list of the Blue-ray characteristics from *Notes from the Cosmos*:

1. Blue Ray Children have dreams that are highly evolved, and they begin dreaming and remembering dreams at a very early age.
2. They have an affinity for languages of all types. Many speak more than one language, if exposed, by age three.
3. They are determined, and at time can be quite stubborn (much like the Indigos).
4. They invent pretending games in which they take on the role of healer, using laying on of hands.
5. They are drawn to water, more than any other setting. They often stare into space at length, especially when near rivers, oceans or even the blue sky.
6. They have an understanding of how animals feel and think. They explain this to others in a matter-of-fact – "Don't you know?"- manner.
7. By the time they reach their teens, many have a desire to go to other countries – often attempting to urge their parents to take them, or going so far as to plan their own trips.
8. Their personalities seem to fluctuate between two extremes – from being serious, single-minded and focused (like the Indigo children), *to being dreamy-eyed and distant* (like the Crystal children).

Doreen Virtue, a leading metaphysical researcher who has been closely involved with the psychic children phenomenon, published a book entitled *The Crystal Children*. According to Virtue, the 'crystals' have been incarnating for only the last seven years, whereas the 'Indigos' and the 'Super-psychics' have been with us for twenty five years and the 'Blue-rays' have been with us for between fifteen and twenty years.

"*Many of the Crystal Children have delayed speech patterns, and it's not uncommon for them to wait until they're three or four years old to begin speaking. However, parents tell me they have no trouble communicating with their silent children – far from it! The parents engage in mind-to-mind communication with their Crystal Children (even before birth). And the Crystals use a combination of telepathy, self-fashioned sign language and sounds (including song), to get their point across."*

This new breed is also often labelled as dysfunctional. Where the Indigo's get labelled with ADD and ADHD, the Crystals are labelled as autistic. Is it just a coincidence that autism is at a record high? An autistic child appears to live in their own world and seem to be disconnected from other people. They do not talk because they are indifferent about communicating with others. Crystal children are quite the opposite. They seem to be very caring and compassionate and continue the traits of the Blue-rays, by showing signs of an ability to heal others. In her previous book on the children, *The Care and Feeding of Indigo Children,* Virtue wrote, *"ADHD should stand for Attention Dialled into a Higher Dimension"*. This would more accurately describe that generation, but in the same vein, Crystal children don't warrant a label of autism; *"they aren't autistic they're AWE-tistic!",* according to Virtue.

"These children are worthy of awe, not labels of dysfunction. If anyone is dysfunctional, it's the systems that aren't accommodating the continuing evolution of the human species. If we shame the children with labels, or medicate them into submission, we will have undermined a heaven-sent gift. **We will crush a civilisation before it has time to take roots".**

This last statement is more profound than was probably intended. These children could be the new 'root race' that is shaping up on planet earth. These children are potentially the new prototype of the human race, and we are the ones who are giving birth to them. Both Gordon Michael Scallion and Edgar Cayce predicted that the fifth root race would appear around the time of the late twentieth century. In *Walking Between the Worlds,* Gregg Braden's research into the Essene texts summarises what a lot of researchers are feeling:

"The ancient texts emphasized that there would be a powerful generation that would be born just before the Shift of the Ages. This generation would have a "force" living within them. Within this force would be a power beyond their knowing. To survive the world that they had created, as well as the challenges that life would offer to them, this last generation would have to reach deep within themselves, to choose the path of love, harmony and compassion. This is the path that would carry them gracefully through the times that the Hopi call the days of "purification", or into the "greatest light" from the Essene perspective. I believe that you and I are witness to that choice. The choice has been made."

One prophet who spoke a similar theme was Mother Shipton. Born Ursula Sontheil in 1488 in Norfolk, England, and who died in 1561, Mother Shipton was a psychic child herself, albeit a very early one. After years of demonstrating prophetic and psychic abilities, she married Toby Shipton and eventually became known as Mother Shipton. Many of her rhyming prophecies came to be in her own lifetime and through the following centuries, but it is this short verse that is relevant here and indicates the times we are in now (2):

> *The children with the second sight*
> *a natural thing so that they might*
> *grow graceful, humble and when they do*
> *the Golden Age will start anew.*

Lets look at this in more detail. '*The children with the second sight*', obviously refers to the psychic ability present in these kids. '*A natural thing*'.. seems to indicate that this is a natural process that humanity goes through. '*So that they might grow graceful (and) humble*': Modern DNA research suggests that the unwinding of DNA is connected to how compassionate and relaxed you can be, which can benefit the DNA helix and leads to a number of positive qualities (see chapter five). '*And when they do the Golden Age will start anew*'; This last line has many possible meanings which we will explore throughout the book. The Essene prophecy, together with this one indicates that a powerful generation of children would appear with great strength before the 'Shift of the Ages'. Both also mention the need to become humble and graceful to 'switch on' these strengths, allowing the light to shine into the darkness.

2. THE HAWAII CONFERENCE

Orion was at my leaving party before I went travelling, where some friends and I were discussing the 'Spoonbenders course' set up by James Twyman on the Internet and how we think it will work. The room fell in to silence and Orion proclaimed, *"There is no spoon"*. The silence blended in to gasps of astonishment as we all had a flashback to the scene in 'The Matrix' movie, where the psychic children say the same line. Orion's Mother confirmed he had not seen the film and when we questioned him as to whether he had seen the film, he confirmed he had not.

So with these experiences in mind, I headed out on my travels with many questions. I had a strong feeling something was going to happen at the Hawaii 'Psychic Children Speak to the World Conference' that was going to change my way of being forever and give me some insights into the phenomenon of the Psychic children. But before I reached the shores of Hawaii, I had time to journey for two and a half months through Mexico and Guatemala, the land of the Maya.

I arrived on a full moon and I made my way to the Thailand of Mexico – Tulum. The beach was stunning. Looking east over the Atlantic deeply moved me. A series of synchronicities led me to the local Tesmescal (sweat lodge). I liked the fact I was starting my three-month journey with a Tesmescal. Ceremonially sweating out all the stress from the flight and emotional trauma of splitting up with my girlfriend a week before. It had to be good? Getting naked in front of other people was a breakthrough for me. Judgements came up when ALL the Americans who were there stripped off a bit too early and had to stand there for thirty minutes whilst the Mayan guy led the ceremony. Very funny. Everybody else stripped off just before getting in the Tesmescal. My very English viewpoint getting the better of me, I realised.

Sweating for nearly three hours is quite intense. I had a candida yeast infection before I went in, but by the time I came out it had either burnt to death or drowned in my internal sweat. Nonetheless it was gone and I was feeling dizzy. We all drank some herb tea and went inside for some porridge. By now I was very hungry and I devoured the porridge. Now, the porridge was extremely sweet. Too sweet. Sweet enough for the remaining Candida to feast on and re-establish their home in my gut. Oh well. Regardless of the day of Candida, the ceremony was important and timely. I felt I was ready for the trek to the pyramids of the Maya.

My journey round the sacred sites of Mexico and Guatemala was an initiation ceremony spread over nearly three months. I already had my ticket for the 'Psychic children' conference in Hawaii, which was scheduled for the spring equinox. I had decided to follow a certain sequence of pyramids through the Yucatan of Mexico and northern Guatemala. The sequence was that of a Fibonacci Spiral that was briefly mentioned by Drunvalo Melchizedek in his *Flower of Life* books. Each site represented a certain chakra and was allegedly built to resonate with that vibration for initiation purposes. I tested this theory by meditating at the sites and feeling which of my chakras was being affected.

The results were interesting and did eventually seem to fit with Drunvalo's theory. For example, when I visited the site at Tulum, I did not know which chakra it was because I couldn't get to a computer and print out the information. I had gotten hold of *another* chakra journey, which did not fit with Drunvalo's. Now it was getting confusing, but I continued none the less. The *other* chakra journey said that Tulum was the second chakra. So I meditated on it. It did not feel like that to me. The Tulum sacred site and the town were very busy places. Much communication was going on. It was a place to share information and a vibrant travelers location. It felt like the throat chakra to me. Definitely, without a doubt. I forgot about this until I got on a computer a few days later and checked Drunvalo's chakra spiral. Yes. It was the throat chakra. I got off to a good start.

The next site that affected me was Chichen Itza. After meditating on the top of the pyramid it became alarmingly clear that this site represented the heart chakra. My heart felt open as soon as I sat down and looked out over the jungle and it stayed like that all the time I was up there. It was quite profound. I felt connected. According to the *other* chakra journey, Chichen Itza was the solar plexus. Hmmmm. I decided to discard this and wait until I got hold of Drunvalo's to confirm my feelings. It was correct. It was the heart chakra. I needed to have my Anahata stimulated it seemed.

Two other things dominated my traveling experience. I had been guided to do certain meditations at the sacred sites to help reconnect with the earth's energy grid – inspired by the work the Psychic children were carrying out. Through the inspiration of James Twyman and some of the children, a global peace meditation had been organized to take place on February 9th. (James Twyman is a peace concert guru who goes off to war-torn places and sings inspirational songs of peace. He is heavily influenced by St. Francis of Assisi and tries to emulate him through selfless action.)

The Great Experiment III involved training the mind and heart to KNOW you can bend a spoon. Not believing it, but KNOWING it. This is the key to successful prayer that has been documented by Gregg Braden in his book *The Isaiah effect*. The build up to this lasted for two weeks playing around with various techniques until you could bend a spoon. There was a great deal of success in this, but Central American spoons are well known for being the thickest in the world! The spoon bending was a sidetrack to the real meaning of the experiment. We had to KNOW world peace.

The day before I went to Uxmal, I had a vivid dream about it. I therefore went in to the site with anticipation and excitement. The pyramid of the magician beckoned me with its curved corners and towering height. There was no way up to the top, but there was a way in. I managed to climb inside and find a quiet spot to meditate. The bats felt my presence as I shone a torch at them and they reminded me that this was part of my initiation as they flew out the exit over my head. Uxmal was an odd place. Its layout looked like some sort of university or school. I felt tired and slept in the shade for a couple of hours until I was woken up by some lizards, who reminded me to pay attention to my dreams. Note taken.

This was not the last of Uxmal. I went back there the next day on a whistle-stop tour around several sites in the area, getting about thirty minutes at each site. I made my way to the pyramid again and meditated sitting on my book about native animal medicine. Within minutes the whistle sounded and I ran to the bus and we headed off to the next site. Aarghh, I'd left my book in the pyramid. What could this mean? It basically meant I had to go back there for a third time. Was the power of Uxmal seducing me back again? Uxmal also means "thrice built" or built over the original pyramid on two later occasions. The significance of visiting Uxmal three times came to me much later and will be discussed in the 'Planetary Grid' chapter.

According to Drunvalo, Uxmal is the 'feminine' center of the planetary grid, whereas the Egyptian pyramids are the 'male' center. The curves on the 'magician' pyramid suggest this feminine link. The chakra journey in the shape of a Fibonacci spiral that I was kind of traveling along, starts at Uxmal (the base chakra) and travels to Labna, Kabah (both were part of the 'whistle-stop' tour), Chichen Itza, Tulum, Kohunlich (near Belize border) and ends at Palenque. Tikal in Guatemala represents the 'next' feminine spiral that continues from Palenque – or to some, the eighth chakra.

After two weeks of travelling through the spiral, the next site that really resonated with me was Tikal, the Mayan mega-city of northern Guatemala. I met a Scotsman called Erland on the bus from Flores and we connected pretty strongly. We arrived just before closing and hurried in to the complex as dusk was falling, but at the main entrance the giant Ceiba tree welcomed us, which was a truly magnificent sight. Ultimately, we found it near impossible to leave the complex and felt magnetised to the central pyramids called Temple I and Temple II in the great plaza. In fact, on the first night there, we got lost in the central plaza and unknowingly circled the pair of pyramids three times. It felt like we were tied by rope to an invisible central point. We decided to adhere to the message we had been given, so we stopped and sat down at the centre, watching the silhouetted pyramids towering over us. Adjusting to the dark we noticed the fireflies on the ground created an imaginary mirror of the stars. It was a sight that I will never forget. Had a spiralling vortex had taken hold and guided us to its centre to see this ancient and timeless view?

The feeling of being lost was getting intense and Erland and I managed to find our way out and find the nearest restaurant. After tucking into our omelettes, two girls entered the café and sat at a table on the other side of the room. They were roughly our age and looked strangely familiar. When a large public space is empty apart from a table with two men at it and a table with two girls, you feel obliged to communicate. So eventually we did, and within minutes we agreed to spend the next night within the pyramid complex of Tikal together. We would spend the daytime 'casing the joint', then stay in the complex until closing time and hide. It was foolproof, but only for the fact that there was a political public relations event on site. We stumbled upon it accidentally, then were trapped when the bell sounded as a signal to leave. The guard guided us out, so we negotiated a bribe that would suit us all. After ten minutes of haggling, we were in.

This is when we realised we had all done this before. I had never had a full blown past life experience before this, so this one was intense. We made our way to the Palace Complex to the south east of the site and eventually got some sleep when the howler monkeys stopped roaring. Michelle was getting a bit scared, so I held her in my arms, so we could get our heads down. She kept waking up in terror, dreaming about what we were doing in our past lives in the palace below us. To cut a long story short, she felt she was a teenage girl, possible of royal origin about a thousand years ago. I was her bodyguard, or possibly her suitor (to be married). Anyway, somewhere along the lines I deserted her and she was kidnapped and possibly killed. She kept getting these images during the proceeding weeks too. We stayed in contact for a few months via e-mail and more revelations kept arising between us.

I only planned to stay at Tikal for a day, but even after my past-life buddies left, I stayed on for another five days. There really is something about Tikal. The experience had really got me. I was in love with this place. It really did feel like home. By the fifth day, I was still not ready to go. The 'Experiment' took hold of me as I circled the city. Unfortunately, it was Sunday and all the locals got in free, so to continue with repetitive prayer and ceremony was a real ego breakdown. Doing 'The Great Experiment III' was a truly liberating feeling.

My journey continued with no time for reflection. After a cooling stop off at Lake Atitlan, Palenque was the next main destination. It was time to feel the highest chakra on the trip. I could not believe anything could top Tikal, and I was right. Palenque was hot and fairly lifeless. Although it was the resting place of Lord Pacal, it did not mesmerize me in any way. I was pining for Tikal. I was missing the roaring howler monkeys and the cool evenings in my hammock. But never mind, it was still an experience in it's own right.

After a brief visit to the pyramids of Teotihuacan, I was on a plane to Hawaii, the final destination on my travels. The Big Island of Hawaii is something else. The energy of this place was potent, almost otherworldly. Whilst collecting my luggage from the airport I was wondering how I was going to get to the beach near the venue in which the conference was being held in. At that moment, a tall, chilled out looking guy approached me and asked me if I had change for a $20 bill. We exchanged notes and I asked him if he knew how I could get to 'Dolphin Bay', on the West coast near Kona. He said, *" I'm driving there now. Wanna lift?"*. I agreed in amazement and we set off on our journey. Within minutes we realized we had the same birthday. What are the chances of that? I felt my time on this island was the start of something special. We stopped off at a health food shop on the way and stocked up on supplies. He then offered to pay for my bill as a welcome present to the Island. I agreed and felt humbled by his generosity. We exchanged numbers and parted company.

Waking up on a beach in Hawaii is usually a very pleasant experience, but occasionally this is not the case. I read that Hawaii only gets a few days of rain per year, but I seemed to be there for *all* of those few rainy days and I was not that well prepared. Anyway, I managed to get to the small bay that the dolphins frequented and swam out about half a mile to play with them. I was in a bit of a mood, through lack of sleep and because I had to walk half a mile to the best spot. The local spinner dolphins did not come near me. They must have sensed my state of being and so avoided me at all costs. I got the message, so when I went back there the next day, I was feeling good and the next thing I know, they were all around me, swimming under me and generally being very playful. Amazing.

GRANDMOTHER CHANDRA

On the day of the spring equinox I met Grandmother Chandra and her telepath friend Saleena Ki in the hotel lobby. Chandra is a 19-year-old multiply handicapped and mute psychic young woman from Arizona who is an expert telepath and was one of the presenters at the conference. Although she is not actually a grandmother, she certainly holds that kind of wisdom and was recognised as a wisdom keeper on the autumn equinox in 1998 when Chief Standing Elk of the Lakota Sioux tribe got a knock on his door that changed his life forever. Here it is in his own words:

There was a beautiful lady standing outside the door, and she said hello, my name is Cat and then she asked me, "Do you know someone by the name of Standing Elk?" I said, "Yes, I'm Standing Elk". Then she said, "My daughter wants to know who this Standing Elk is, because he kept her up all night playing his flute, singing and making her dance. She came to find out who he is." I asked her, "Is she with you?"

She said "yes." I asked her to bring her in. In a few minutes she entered the house with this beautiful young woman. She carried her into the living room placed her gently on the couch. There she sat, so innocent and beautiful and she began "looking around" and feeling the spirit and atmosphere of the energy around her. She said (via telepathy), "I want to talk to Standing Elk!"

I immediately said, "I know you! You are my grandmother!" She said "Yes, Yes, Yes!" She said, "I want to know about the Universal and Spiritual Laws of Creator". I told her, "You already know them". She said "Yes, Yes, Yes!" Then she asked me, "Why am I like this? I cannot do anything with my body, but my mind is perfect! Why? What is my purpose here?"

I told her, "You are to teach the Universal and Spiritual Laws of Creator. The reason you are the way you are is because of the effect you will have on mankind. We are the ones that failed to communicate with the children, we don't have time for the children with the problems that you have physically. Instead we stick them in hospitals and institutions and let them wither away. We need to help the people understand that we can communicate now. Thanks to the efforts of your Mother, Cat. She has opened the doors for the parents to learn that gift of sacred communication with their children."

She said, "Yes, Yes, Yes! (1)*"*

They continued to communicate telepathically and she named herself 'Screaming Eagle' and was also initiated to be one of their nation's 'Pipe Carriers'. She chose the name because when the eagle screams, it tells the truth. Chandra also claims to have retained all the knowledge from her past lives and is able to communicate with dolphins, whales and ET's. She even told the audience at the conference that she was not human, but a 12th dimensional ET! An example of wisdom from Chandra appeared in one of James Twyman's emails in early 2002. I just have to share what she said:

"The psychic children are portals or gateways that spread peace upon the earth. They are in different areas to open the earth's grids for the ascended masters to come through and bring peace consciousness to the planet. These children have special vision and have contracted to come to earth at this time. There is a belief in a tremendous battle between the light and dark forces now. Those who are aligned with peace will follow the children. There will be a great ascension into the Light by the people of the earth as well as the planetary ascension to the next level of consciousness ...all is just an illusion we have created because we have refused to rip away the veils to see what is real". (2).

Chandra aged 19 with Mother, Cat (grandmchandra.com)

THE 'LEMURIA' CEREMONY

After connecting with Chandra, she allowed me to join her for a 'Stargate opening ceremony', located in a residential area of Waikaloa near Mauna Kea In North Hawaii. We drove in two cars to the location. Chandra and her telepathic interpreter were in the front car, whilst the rest of us were in the following car. In turn, each person felt Chandra communicating with them telepathically. All I felt was a pressure in my head, obviously not quite attuned to the telepathic realm yet.

After carrying Chandra in my arms to the right spot on the hill, we quickly concluded the ceremony. The energy was felt by all as it circulated around the thirteen of us. According to Chandra this ceremony was part of a sequence of events that finally released and reactivated the ancient land of Lemuria, which is where the Big Island of Hawaii now stands. This bit of 'new-agey' information really got under my skin. Initially I thought nothing of it, believing it was over active imaginations, but strange things started happening throughout the conference that supported this.

The thirteen of us who participated in the ceremony had supposedly helped the souls that were trapped in the Lemuria cataclysm to become free and be released through the conference. Some people felt that all the people at the conference were once Lemurians. People kept being tapped on the shoulder and heard voices in their ear, only to find out no one was behind them! According to Saleena Ki, we witnessed and assisted the landing of the Light body of Lemuria on top of the physical body of The Big Island of Hawaii and anchored it again. It seems that throughout the conference, many different people were called to participate in archetypal roles in the sequence of events that lead up to the full restoration of Lemuria. When Grandmother Chandra was asked what this means in the real world, she asked us to feel into our hearts and see how open and easy the channels of love were now. So what to make of all this? Was it new-age ideas taking over our consciousness, or is there really something in this?

The ceremony took place on March 20th at 3pm, which was the spring equinox, the astrological transition to Aries and the Mayan New Year. Some notable events had already been experienced on the island. Saleena told me that on 3/3/03 - the Christ and Mary consciousness (which also seemed to represent the divine feminine and the divine masculine) merged. On 8/3/03 - this newly merged consciousness, then merged with the dolphin and whale consciousness. And on 11/3/03, a stargate called NAAM was opened which strengthened the earth's energy grid, which the children have been working with for some years. You might be wondering how all this ceremonial stuff seems to work. Well, Saleena told me that Hawaii is 19.5 degrees below the equator and is a major point on the earth's energy grid, which allows this sort of work to be very potent. The energy at this point in Hawaii connects with other points around the planet through lines of force that bind the structure of the earth together.

Hawaii is intense. The veil feels very thin. So much so, you can often catch glimpses of spirits out of the corner of your eye. I could barely sleep the whole time I was on the Big Island of Hawaii. The Psychic children chose this location for the conference because they needed to be here to work on this node-point of the global energy grid at this particular time (the spring equinox).

HAWAII & THE STAR TETRAHEDRON

Hawaii is an interesting place to start on the planetary grid. The islands of Hawaii sit at 19.47 degrees (rounded off to 19.5) below the equator that was first documented by Richard Hoagland in his classic work, *The Monuments of Mars: City on the Edge of Forever*. In the early 1990's the former NASA scientist had become intrigued by what appeared, in NASA photographs, to be a number of pyramids and a humanoid face clustered together in a region called Cydonia on the surface of Mars. As his research continued he recognized that Cydonia sits just north of the 19.5-degree latitude on Mars, with the Olympus Mons, a shield volcano that is three times the size of Mount Everest, at the 19.5 degree point. Hoagland decided to use his knowledge of geometry and placed a tetrahedron (three sided pyramid) inside a sphere and found a correspondence (3).

Jupiter's red spot and Moon

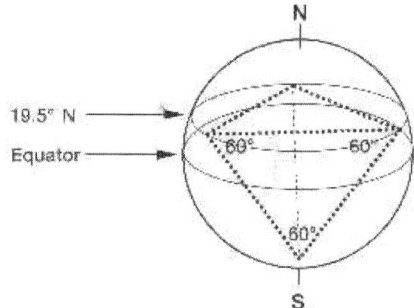
Tetrahedral geometry in a sphere

He checked all the planets in the solar system for similar anomalies and found that most of them had 'something of interest' at 19.5 degrees – either above or below the equator, depending on which way up he placed the tetrahedron. He found that 'energy upwellings' were also present at sites on earth, with the volcanoes of Hawaii. On the Sun was regular sunspot activity that never drifts from around 19.5 degrees north or south. As we head out to the more gaseous planets, spiralling energetic effects become apparent. The massive constant-storm that is Jupiter's red-spot sits at this degree south; as does its orbiting moon. This can be seen in this convenient image above.

Neptune shows a dark spot like Jupiter and rotating cloud bands at the same geometry, whilst Venus has a double volcano at the same latitude. On Saturn there are dark bands of clouds at 19.5 degrees north and south of the equator. This indicates that interlocking tetrahedra are energetically present.

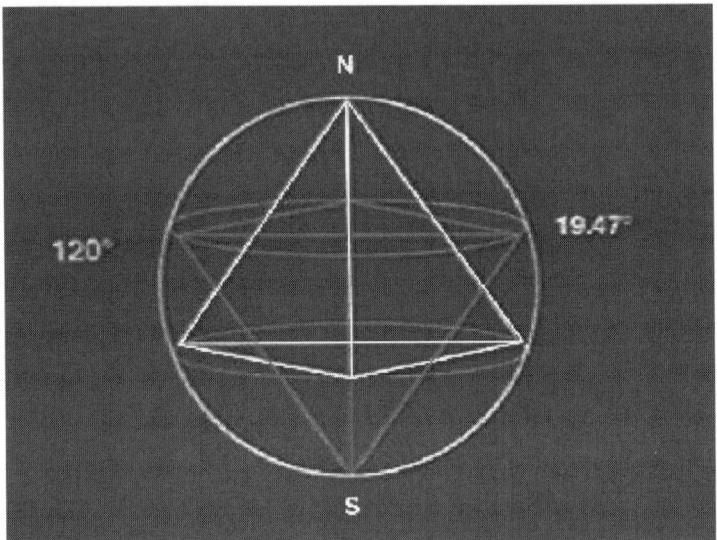

Interlocking star-tetrahedron inside a sphere, showing coordinate points (Hoagland 2000)

The star tetrahedron is significant because it is one of the shapes that energetic inter-dimensional vehicles, known as the 'Merkaba' or 'Light-body', manifests as. At planet earth's 19.5-degree latitude we have the intersection between the light-body of the planet with its surface. Being at one of these sites during a solstice or equinox, we have the potential to experience the earth's 'light body' first hand and through intention and concentration beneficial grid-work can be carried out. This is why the ceremonies with Chandra were said to be 'successful'. The spiralling uprisings on the gaseous planets give us a clue to the nature of this energy within a planet and how it streams in and out from the surface of the earth. American mystic Linda Lemuria repeatedly caught this on camera at the 'star-gate' in North Hawaii, where the photos showed uprising blocks of red and orange energy.

STARGATES

Before we get into the grid, we need to know exactly what a stargate is, because these are its main access points. A stargate is an etheric inter-dimensional energy alignment between two points in space, which allows high vibrational energies to pass across long distances. Put simply, it is a sub-space vortex that energy passes through. This passage of energy is unrestricted during a solstice or equinox, when the position of the planet is such as to allow an optimal amount of energy through to earth. During a stargate ceremony, cosmic energy is brought into the earth through a meditation and conscious intention. Participants act as "conductors", by connecting their physical bodies and conscious mind to the energies coming to the planet. New and enlightening information may be brought to the earth this way. During a stargate ceremony important 'earth work' may also be performed, such as the alignment of the earth's energy grids, which is what we were doing at the Hawaii stargate.

Stargate alignments are particularly crucial at this time, as the vibration of the earth is speeding up as we continue to move through an area of highly charged space. Stargates allow high vibrational interstellar energies to permeate the grids of the earth with ease and grace, and in doing so allow the energies to fully integrate into the etheric and energetic grid structures of the planet. As we are also connected to the grids and the earth, it serves as a chance for spiritual growth within the individual as these high-vibrational energies permeate our own energy matrix and can influence DNA mutation and higher states of consciousness. Hunbatz Men, Mayan elder and modern day-keeper, suggests getting out to sacred sites on the grid to correct an ancient a flaw in human DNA. He believes this will also strengthen our energy bodies for the coming transition at the end of the Great Cycle (4).

There are many stargates around the earth and many new ones are appearing as the energetic structure of the earth is changing. Stone circles, pyramids, hill-tops and sacred sites all over the world are recognised as stargates, but as humans, we need to step in and become the new conductors for this higher form of energy. These 'node-points' around the planet have been mapped out by such visionaries as Bruce Cathie, Richard Hoagland and the team of Becker and Hagens, but as we will see later, this work does not only need to be carried out at 'points' on the grid.

VORTEX PHENOMENA

The vortex phenomenon that happens at these sites depends on certain solar, astronomical and galactic frequencies. Sometimes there is more energy coming into the earth, when grid-work can be most effective. At other times the energy is streaming out from the earth, usually through these node-points. An example of the latter was when a group of people were camped inside Stonehenge and the stones were struck by lightning. Witnesses saw them all disappear, leaving only their charred tent pegs (5). David Wilcock believes that the higher energy vibration of the lightning activated the vortex that Stonehenge had been built to harness, which in turn caused this to happen. He also believed this enabled the builders of the monument to travel through space and time.

Major F.A.Menzies, a distinguished British Army engineer and surveyor in the First World War, witnessed a similar event. He moved to

France to study earth energies and the Feng Shui system of geomancy and by the nineteen-forties he was an established geomancer, able to locate ley lines and advise on ill health caused by geopathic stress. One day, when he was at the 5,000 year old megalithic site, Stanton Drew, just south of Bristol in England, he had an extraordinary 'stargate' experience which was later related to fellow surveyor, George Sandwich in 1952, a year before his death:

"Although the weather was dull there was no sign of a storm. Just at a moment when I was re-checking a bearing on one of the stones in that group, it was as if a powerful flash of lightning hit the stone, so the whole group was flood-lit, making them glow like molten gold in a furnace. Rooted to the spot – unable to move – I became profoundly awestruck, as dazzling radiations from above, caused the whole group of stones to pulsate with energy in a way that was terrifying. Before my eyes, it seemed the stones were enveloped in a moving pillar of fire – radiating light without heat – writhing upwards towards the heavens: on the other hand it was descending in a vivid spiral effect of various shades of colour – earthward. In fact the moving, flaring lights gyrating around the stones had joined the heavens with the earth". (6)

Menzies is recounting vortex phenomena that, in similar forms, has been witnessed at various sacred sites and known stargates. The ceremony that Chandra and I were a part of in Hawaii, although occasionally caught on camera, had no such brilliant light phenomena, but these reports demonstrate the type of powerful energy we are dealing with here. His account also gave an example of how the earth's energy connects with the energy of the cosmos.

THE HAWAII CONFERENCE

The pre-conference concert coincided with the first bombs being dropped on Iraq. The date was March 20th 2003. The polarity of being at a beautiful conference in paradise on one side of the earth, whilst destruction and madness began on the other, emphasized the importance that these gatherings have. The awareness and power of group consciousness has been a major teaching of the children and of James Twyman, who between them organise global peace meditations via the Internet. Some of you might have been involved in The Great Experiment III, which happened on February 9th 2003. About 100,000 people did this one focusing on the trouble in Israel when things were really kicking off.

Makia Malo, an Hawaian storyteller and poet, opened the proceedings with a 'special' chant written for the conference. It translated to something like this:

In the eyes of the sacred we are one
Each of us one blossom in this Kona garland,
Now invited by the sacred go forth
And weave others into this, Lei of peace.

The rest of the concert seemed like a Mount Shasta reunion with Anton Mizerak, Matisha, and his annoying 'channelled' character, Dolphinanda, a cross between Mickey Rooney and Mickey Mouse. The children were briefly introduced, but the highlight of the night was when the power blew and an Aum started spontaneously. Aaaahhh.

The following day, after brief introductions from James Twyman and some cheesy keyboard music, Natasa-La took the stage. The twenty year old recounted experiences of her life as a psychic child. She also had a 'teacher' quality about her and a depth of compassion towards many of the children who are very sensitive. She emphasised that when we are dealing with the new children, that we must stay heart-centred and open-minded, to be able to empathise with them.

"The Psychic children are here to raise our vibration and change our DNA. They teach us about love and they require tremendous patience as they have problems adjusting to this world. They are very clear about their missions, which may clash with our expectations of them. This can lead to incredible outbursts of anger, but when this happens, we are advised to step back and remember who we truly are. When we can embrace our divinity, honour ourselves, and find that calm space within, we can embrace them better. Easier said than done, but this does work! Each day is extremely important for psychic children to ground and physically connect with the earth. Listen to and support them, even if you don't understand them. Be open with them, show you want to learn from them and that you treat them equal in your communications. More than anything else, they need our unconditional love and a way of showing this, is by bathing them in pink and lavender light".

Although Grandmother Chandra was not in the room, she showed off her telepathic skills from her hotel room. She was extremely tired and drained from all the travelling and the ceremony that she had coordinated. Her telepathic interpreter Saleena Ki, stood in for her on stage and shared these words:

"At this moment in time there is an ark of dolphins on the coast all pointing towards the hotel. The whales are creating sacred geometry grids in deep waters. We are all supported by the dolphins and the whales. They do the same work under water as we are doing on earth, and remember, they are the true guardians of the earth, not us. There are sparkles of lavender light, like rain, above us from the Angelic realms. They are taking a break and supporting the conference. We are all also helping them in some way.

Next up was a short video called 'Grapevine Galore', that demonstrated how thirty Korean school children were trained within three days and developed skills in telepathy, clairvoyance and even X-ray vision. The results were fascinating, showing how the unconditioned mind can easily pick up these qualities. Chi-kung and breathing exercises were also part of the training, and left the audience realising that we are all potentially psychic, but we have suppressed our abilities in order to conform to social expectations.

Before the lunch break, Zach, an eleven-year-old from Mount Shasta spoke for a few minutes about the need for personal peace;

"If you have peace within yourself, you see peace in everything. Do peaceful acts every day and be helpful at all times. Do anything you can to help anybody, because something as small as a beetle could have been your Mother in a past life. Treat the earth nice, like a mother or a grandmother....we need to build up peace within to get the peace outside."

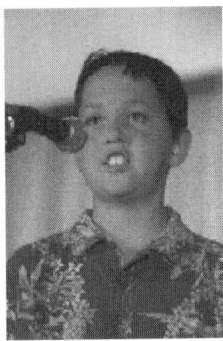
Zach

Koya and James Twyman (emissaryoflight.com)

From the age of three Zach was communicating telepathically with other kids from all over the world. Michael, a Chinese psychic kept 'calling', even though he spoke a different language. By being *"tuned to a higher frequency"*, the global telepathic network of these kids transcends this language barrier. (This has also been explored in the 'Indigo' film)

Dolphin and whale researcher Joan Ocean's first six words instigated a cheer from the audience - *"Play is more important than work. Play is the source of life renewal. The whales spend 60-70% of their time playing, so must we"*. Joan Ocean has spent many years working with these beautiful creatures. She is an Hawaiian resident who has developed a strong bond with the local dolphins and whales and has devised a way to communicate with them.

Koya (meaning 'I am light'), a disabled and mute five-year-old child from Japan continued this message of play; *"Having fun is very important to us. If you are not having fun, your consciousness flows to a not so nice place, so please do all the fun joy things you can ever do"*. He continued through his letter board and interpreter:

"All the disabled children are smart. All of us. We have a role to play. We have come to earth for a certain role or purpose. People try to blame the

Mother, but this is not right, we decided to be born like this. I have a special God. I talk to God every day and I chose this. I promised that I would bring peace to the world. This is my purpose".

On the subject of war, Koya had this to say.

"It's important for us to become One mind, to become One. That is all we can do, but we will never give up. Someday the world will be One. I know it will come. The time is close....really! I will never forget when we all prayed on February 9th. Everybody in the world was meditating, weren't they? I felt so much light. It was so bright, like me! Everyone was shining. Just like me. The day when we will have fun love is getting closer. Love will be victorious in the end. Remember...I am light and so are you."

The final speaker of the day was Lizzie, whose philosophy is summed up in four words; *"Wish. Pray. Dream. Have".* She explained, *"Set your intentions and they will manifest quickly if you are guided by your heart. Wish for peace and love, pray for it, then it becomes part of you, you dream about it, then you have it, it has become your reality".* At two years old Lizzie could see the spirits of dead children ('The Sixth Sense' movie anyone?) and after communing with them for some time she learnt how to help them through to the other side. She has helped many since then, but life has not been so easy for Lizzie. Twice she has gone blind. At one time, a green ball of light entered her eyes when she was in the woods with Zach and completely blinded her. Nevertheless, on both occasions she eventually regained her eyesight. Grandmother Chandra had the final words of wisdom.

"Connect with Metatron and Melchizedek, they are working with us now". Someone asked about what we can do to help. Chandra replied, *"Help yourself by spinning 33 times in a clockwise direction. Look at your right thumb and use a point in the room to count. When you finish push your palms together strongly to stop you falling over. This is very important. We must connect to the crystal grid that has been set up. Focus your intentions and join with it. The dodecahedron in sacred geometry will help with understanding the alignments. We must be in a place of heart and keep our heart and feet chakras open or we will feel pain in our body. We must not hide from ourselves or from others. WE MUST REVEAL OURSELVES TO GROW. I will visit you in your dreams, we have much work to do in the dreamtime. Plus make sure you pay attention to the whales, the dolphins and the water – there are many keys there".*

The conference succeeded in downloading the most important knowledge from a selection of the more well-known psychic children, and gave the attendee's an insight into their world. It was Chandra's messages about the planetary grid that really got me going. It made perfect sense why I could barely sleep when I was in Hawaii. It was a point on the grid and with the information about stargates and Lemuria repeating over in my mind it triggered a research project into this subject. I felt the grid was not only 'managed' by humans. I had a feeling our underwater friends were in on it too.

It was on my last day in Hawaii that I got some answers regarding my feelings when I was invited to the stargate near Linda Lemuria's house. I was the only man there and there were seven women. After the ceremony we all sat down and started sharing stories. One of the stories I heard happened only two days ago and only two miles up the coast from Kona. Three of the women who I shared the ceremony with informed me that they had personally seen several UFOs move erratically in the sky for a few minutes, then entered the sea in an area known to be a resting place of the whales! But these women didn't seem shocked in any way. They had all seen it happen before. Linda Lemuria reminded me that most ET's do not bother communicating with us humans; they just go straight to the whales and the dolphins – the true keepers of the planet.

THOMAS & THE WHALES

There is a true story about two pods of whales on opposite sides of the planet during late July 2002. It was widely reported that in Sydney Harbour, a group of whales performed to onlookers for hours. At precisely the same time, the same number of whales beached themselves on the coast of Cape Cod in America. Most of these whales died. So what did the Bulgarian psychic child Thomas feel about this in his mass-email he sent out:

"We still have time! The universe is trying to show us that we have a choice. Which will we choose? The fact that these two things happened at the same time in different parts of the world tells us that humanity has a unique opportunity. We stand on the brink of a "choice point," which means that two different worlds are existing side by side, and our emotions will decide which will remain.

The scientists of the world have been speaking of these "choice points" for many years, though one such as this is very rare. The impact of our choice is beyond anything we can describe. All we can say is that your choice will reveal the path you will walk toward Grace and Enlightenment. The path may be difficult or it may be peaceful. It is up to you. The work the Children are doing right now is meant to make that shift peaceful, but the result will be the same either way. That is why fear is not appropriate, but caution is. You have an important role to play in choosing which of these two experiences will rule. Think of the whales for a moment. One group gave its life to reveal the impact of our choices.

Will their lives be given in vain? The other group took a step toward humanity, showing what is possible if we make the choice of peace. Do you remember when we [the Psychic Children] told you how you will be able to tell which path humanity has chosen? If the whales and dolphins begin interacting with humans in closer ways, then you will know you have chosen well. But if they retreat and die, then you will know that the road ahead will be very difficult. But your success is assured because the Truth cannot be denied forever. We only ask that you choose well, for today's children and tomorrow's. If you choose peace now and allow your minds to flow into that reality, then the political systems will adjust on their own, and you will see the results of that in the world. Your emotions are the key. It is the tool you will use to draw the chosen world into your conscious experience. Your collective emotions have the ability to influence weather patterns and even end wars. You have done this many times without realizing it. If you continue claiming the world you want by "feeling" that world in your emotions, then it will be so. But if you continue to be influenced by the fear that is so present today, then the world will reflect that as well. We, your Children, are asking you to choose love over fear.

Then the whales and the dolphins will fulfil their role and give us back the information they store within each cell. It is so important that this happen. The circle of life cannot be broken now. Use your feelings of love to draw the reality you really want. We still have more to share.

We love you, Thomas "

THE 'DOLPHIN' CROP CIRCLE

Thomas' messages did not end there. Within weeks something appeared in the fields of England that invited another message from this amazing child. On August 14th 2002, at exactly the same time Thomas was sending us his warning about the low frequency sonar that is beginning to destroy ocean mammals all over the world, a crop circle of dolphins surrounding the Earth appeared in Alton Barnes in Wiltshire. It clearly shows two dolphins surrounding a small sphere, with three circles around that sphere. It looks a lot like dolphins symbolically protecting the earth and three 'grids' that are being strengthened around it. Check it out for yourself.

'Dolphin' Crop circle, Alton Barnes, August 14th 2002 (cropcircleconnector.com)

From Thomas: "*Are you surprised that this information is being presented to you in this new way? These crop circles are communicating with your inner mind, and the message is clear. The Psychic Children have been telling you that we stand at the brink of an incredible awakening, and that the dolphins and whales play a critical role. Why, then, are we trying to destroy them, so that we won't have to hear their message or receive their Gift? The deployment of the low frequency sonar is how you have chosen to close your ears to their Gift, and to their cries for help. Why else would you seek to destroy their hearing, causing them to beach themselves and die? This is a wake up call, and it is not just from the Children, or even the dolphins and whales. Now it is coming from your brothers and sisters from other dimensions and planets.*

That is why this dolphin crop circle was revealed at exactly the same time these messages are being distributed. What will you do? Will you open your heart and become part of the creative solution? Or will you turn the other way, even though there are so many who are trying to snare your attention? This is the moment you must decide. The Children are pulling humanity to the next level in its evolution, but only if you allow it. There is a code in this crop circle that only your super-conscious mind will comprehend. It may reveal your own role, how you can contribute to the world of peace and compassion.

It is so important that people all over the world see this crop circle, for it will activate you in ways your mind cannot understand. Please send this e-mail to everyone you can so others will be activated as well. It is so

important.
This is the time you must respond.

We love you, Thomas "

Psychic children and crop circles are intimately linked. In Holland, there were reports of a young boy called Robert Van der Broeke (now in his twenties) who regularly made crop circles in the field behind his house (see bltresearch.com). There are ongoing poltergeist phenomena in his house as well, which many researchers believe is linked to the psychic power of children at around the age of puberty. When I look at many of the 'playful' designs of crop formations, I often do wonder if children were involved in the design. The dolphin formation definitely has a child-like quality to it.

3. THE PLANETARY GRID

When New Zealand airline pilot, Bruce Cathie was regularly out flying planes and spending time on boats he kept seeing UFOs. By 1965 he realised there was a pattern emerging as to the flight paths of these crafts. He became fascinated by this and soon discovered the UFOs were indeed following straight-line paths. He mapped them out and found a 'grid system' over New Zealand and the surrounding ocean. This led him to the realisation that the entire earth had this 'grid'.

Cathie is not a trained scientist or mathematician, but upon reading his work, you can tell he has an advanced understanding of his subject. In fact his work was so far ahead of his time that several government agencies have offered him millions of dollars to sell them his research and to keep his mouth shut about his ongoing discoveries.

A French researcher by the name of Aime Michel had been carrying out similar work in Europe. He had found that the distances between parallel flight-paths were estimated at 54.46 kilometres. Converted to nautical miles, Cathie discovered that the paths were exactly thirty nautical miles apart [1]. One nautical mile is exactly one minute of arc on the earth's surface; therefore sixty nautical miles would be one degree of arc. There are 360 degrees in a circle or sphere, so what we have here is a harmonic between the earth's energy grid and the shape of the sphere – the earth itself! Cathie checked his discovery with many other UFO researchers and found that his theory was being taken seriously, much to the dislike of the people who were trying to buy his research.

David Wilcock was the first to point out that Cathie had unknowingly discovered the cube and octahedron inside a sphere – two of the stages of the sequence of platonic solids of the Grid (see on p.33-35).

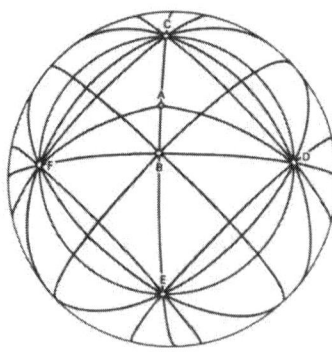

Cubeoctahedron inside a sphere

The 'Aerial' 13,500 feet deep in the ocean

The oceans held the next stage of his global-grid formula. He had noticed that many reports of UFO's entering the sea at certain locations. He put these locations onto his grid-map and found them to be crossing points on the grid. But it was a photograph of an unknown structure 13,500 feet deep off the coast of Cape Horn in South America that really caught his attention. It appeared to be a metal antenna of some sort with geometrically placed bars protruding out from it at certain angles. He checked his grid-map and found that this was also a major crossing point and that the direction of the bars corresponded with the direction of the grid lines. This piece of information and his research up to that point allowed him to form a detailed version of the grid he had discovered.

The mysterious underwater structure and sightings of UFOs entering the ocean link with the research of dolphin researcher Joan Ocean, who spoke at the psychic children conference. She says that the government's sonar experiments disrupted the electro-magnetic lines of the earth so that the UFOs could no longer navigate our oceans. It also suggests that there are indeed underwater bases set up by ET's. Cathie also once saw a fast-horizontal moving UFO 'fire' a glowing rod into the sea at a precise vertical angle. He concluded that the UFO had aimed the rod at a particular point on the ocean floor, which could be linked to the 'aerial' found at Cape Horn.

80% of the world's oceans were having sonar pumped through them to supposedly scan for enemy submarines! But why does America need to scan almost the entire earth. Surely just around the coast of their own country is more appropriate. Thomas's message brought this to mass awareness and helped in bringing these experiments to a close. Joan Ocean knew all about the experiments long before they were put into practice.

"In March 1998 the US Navy performed testing of the LFAS system off the shores of Kona, Hawaii. Groups from our community mounted a protest by finding the Navy vessel, the Corey Chouest, and entering into the water to prevent them from using the sonar array. The fact that they could not use this system while a human was in the water within two miles, is a clue as to it's inherent danger to dolphins and whales who are more than ten times as sensitive to this proven lethal technology (2)."

In fact, according to David Phillips, Director of Earth Island Institute's International Marine Mammal Project, *"The Navy's Low Frequency Active (LFA) Sonar system has the potential to deafen every marine mammal living in the world's oceans"*. It was apparently the equivalent of standing right next to a Saturn-V rocket take-off. The federal National Marine Fisheries Service (NMFS) approved the granting of "small take" permits to kill and harass whales and other endangered species for the U.S. Navy's Low Frequency Active (LFA) Sonar. But was this the real reason behind the experiments? Not according to Joan Ocean:

"Through my on-going communications with the dolphins and whales, I have learned that this sonar weaponry is being deployed worldwide to prevent our brothers and sisters from neighbouring planets from traversing Earth's oceans. This may sound unusual to some people, but it seems that the 'E.T.s' are considered 'the enemy.' I know a number of military personnel who have personally witnessed and detected with radar, the ultra-advanced spaceships entering and leaving the ocean. Certain large-brained whales such as the Humpbacks and Sperm whales are in contact with these off-worlders who frequent our oceans and are here by invitation."

Joan Ocean confirmed what I heard on my last day in Hawaii. The 'off-worlders' are in contact with the whales – the true keepers of the planet and possibly the intelligence behind the maintenance of the grid. If whales can form huge geometric designs in deep waters, they obviously have some knowledge of basic sacred geometry. It also feels like the whales and dolphins are in cahoots with the psychic children. This is why Hawaii was chosen for the conference. They underwater beings were listening in too.

THE PLATONIC SOLIDS

The five Platonic solids hold the key to understanding the planetary grid system. Already we have seen that the cube and octahedron are present in Cathie's work. Hoagland unlocked the star-tetrahedron, so now we only need to find the icosahedron and the dodecahedron. Here is a diagram of the Platonic solids in a sequence that relates to the progression of vibration, the ancient Indian theory of how they correspond to the colours of the rainbow spectrum, and also the notes in a 'pure diatonic' scale. Therefore what they are really showing us is the dimensions we, and the Universe are slowly travelling through. We are currently in the 'Octahedron' or 'Third' dimension/density and will soon be moving into the 'Star-Tetrahedron' or 'fourth' dimension/density.

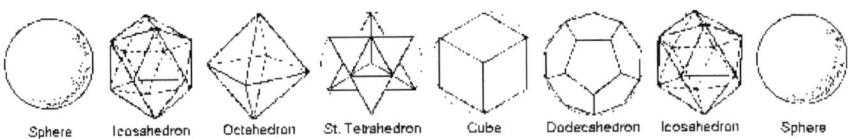

Sphere   Icosahedron   Octahedron   St. Tetrahedron   Cube   Dodecahedron   Icosahedron   Sphere

The 'Octave' of Platonic Solids (Wilcock 1999)

Research from Dr. Hans Jenny has demonstrated that vibration produces geometry. By creating vibration in a material that we can see, the pattern of the vibration becomes visible in the medium. Through experiments conducted in a variety of substances, Dr. Jenny produced an amazing variety of geometric patterns, ranging from very complex to very simple. In such materials as water, oil, graphite and sulphur powder, each pattern was simply the visible form of an invisible force. He called it *Cymatics*. These geometric patterns have a three-dimensional structure and through careful inspection show us the geometries of the Platonic solids according to the sequence of musical vibration shown in the above image. Sound actually has a recognized form to it that is a geometric design. This design has depth, length and height to its structure. This is why the Tibetans refer to geometry as "frozen sound". The mandalas that ancient cultures used are two-dimensional patterns that represent three-dimensional sound.

The earliest known use of the Platonic geometries (or Polyhedra – literally meaning *'many seats'*) goes back to the Neolithic cultures of Britain – not Plato. The Ashmolean Museum in Oxford has several hand-sized stones that show precise geometries of the five known solids. In *Time Stands Still,* Keith Critchlow conservatively estimates them to be 2400 years old – 1000 years before Plato, but other archaeological researchers date them to 20,000 BC (*Jeffrey Goldman & Robert Cowley – independent archaeologists*). Although other researchers suggest they were used as projectiles in hunting and warfare, Critchlow determined that they were more likely to have been used for the study, comparison, and analysis of spherically determined systems of geometry, including, perhaps for the mapping and study of the planetary grid.

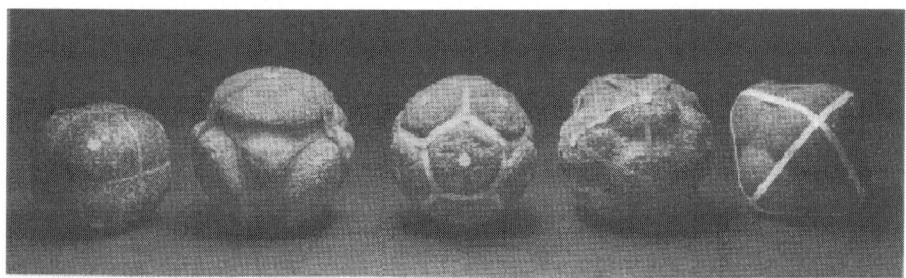

Plato famously wrote, *"The earth, viewed from above, resembles a ball sewn from twelve pieces of skin"*. This would describe the dodecahedron, but he mysteriously left out the name of this *"certain fifth composition"*, which simply seems to be this form. Plato's account of four of the solids and how they relate to the elements was documented in the *Timaeus,* which described four of the shapes with the four elements. Fire – Tetrahedron, Air – Octahedron, Earth – Cube, Water – Icosahedron. There were also rumours that if the dodecahedron were mentioned in the ancient mystery schools, that person would be executed. I postulate that it was not the dodecahedron that would get a man killed, but a certain combination of *all* the Platonic solids into one unified whole that resembled a dodecahedron. By the end of this chapter we will see if it was this he was referring to.

THE ICOSAHEDRON GRID

There are twenty faces on the icosahedron, with twelve outer points that Ivan P. Sanderson, a paranormal researcher, found were linked to locations where very strange phenomena such as loss of time and disappearances have taken place (4). The Bermuda Triangle is one of these 'Vile-Vortices' and so is an area off the coast of Hawaii. The image below shows the direction of the electro-magnetic forces that this grid regulates.

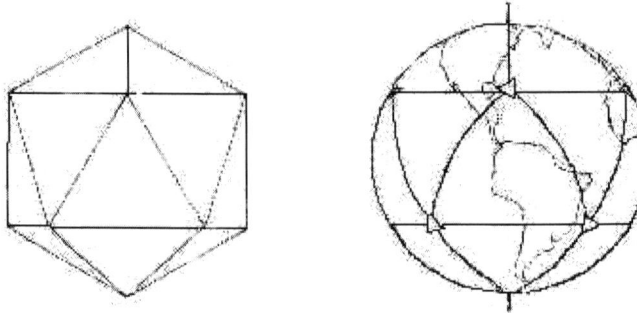

The Icosahedron Grid (Wilcock 2000)

THE GREAT PYRAMID

The Greenwich meridian is dictating time all over the planet. All clocks, navigation and time zones are set from this north-south line. If we shift the Greenwich Meridian about 31 degrees east, it rests on the north-south line of the Great Pyramid, its original site. Through extensive research, archeocryptographer Carl Munck, rediscovered that the north-south line through Egypt is the *original* prime meridian of the planet. Not only is it the place on earth where the most land mass surrounds it in varying directions (as discovered by Professor Charles Piazzi Smyth in 1884); it is also the only point where all the grids meet. The importance of Egypt being re-established as the Prime Meridian is essential if we are to have any chance of helping the earth rebalance herself.

Through his study of the entire planet he found that the original prime meridian, where *all* co-ordinates were taken from was on the north-south line that went through the Great Pyramid. All the sacred sites on his grid of coordinates were mapped out by using this as their base line. The Greenwich Meridian is only a later construct and is well off the correct alignment. Tikal and the underwater pyramid in Wisconsin also follow a similar north-south alignment (5).

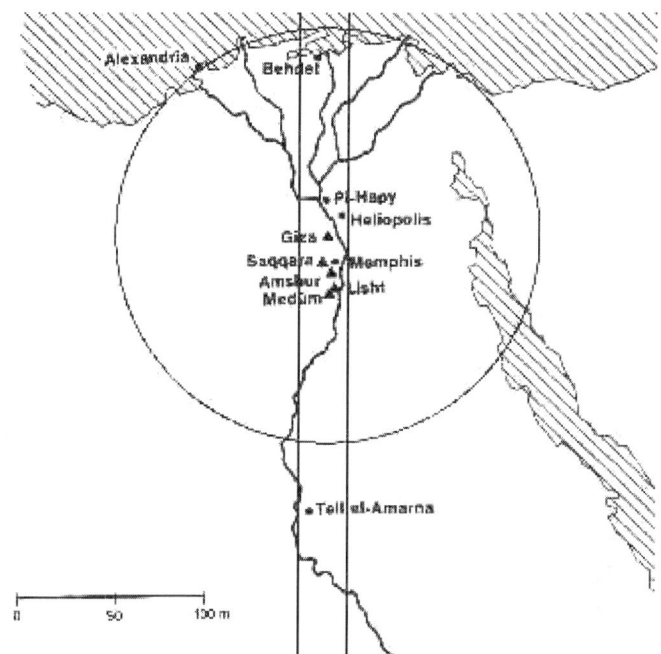

Notice how ALL the pyramids of Egypt are on this 20-mile wide line.

The Great Pyramid is built over the single most powerful vortex on the planet, where the lines of the tetrahedron, cube, octahedron, icosahedron and the dodecahedron grids all cross. Wilcock believes that it had to be built there, because it is the gravitational balance point of the world's continents (6). He also states that the geometries of the grids needed a point to work from and this point is where the Great Pyramid is located. It is as though it is a plug that balances the earth's energy structure, regulates cosmic frequencies to and from the earth and is the 'centre' in earth grid research (7).

    The harmonic locations of megalithic structures can be demonstrated if we look at numerous sacred sites in relation to this longitude. Many sites fall into simple harmonic fractions of the sphere; for example –140 degrees West we get Easter Island; 130 degrees West we get Teotihuacan and Tula in Mexico; Lhasa, the Tibetan capital is 60 degrees East. But what we need to focus on is the tetrahedron within the sphere – sites that are 120 east and west of the Giza meridian. 120 degrees West we get the Central American Mayan sites of Copan, Quirigua, Tikal, Uxmal and Lubaantum (where the Mitchell-Hedges crystal skull was discovered in 1927) (8) ; 120 degrees east we get the submerged ruins of Yonaguni, off the southern coast of Japan – that is at least 12,000 years old according to Graham Hancock.

    So we know that the tetrahedron has three main areas touching the surface of the earth (with the fourth point at the pole). Each 120 degrees from each other (360 degrees is the sphere), but there seems to be a problem regarding this star-tetrahedron point being in Hawaii, due to the prime meridian being in Egypt. If this is the correct prime meridian, the Hawaii alignment does not fit. Although there is a slight anomaly with this idea, by the end of this chapter we will see that although Hawaii is perhaps not part of this particular configuration, it is in fact a 'major node-point' on the most accurate version of the main planetary grid.

When we travel 120 degrees west from Giza, we meet the area of the Mexican and Guatemalan pyramids. Although they are not directly on the 'point' of 19.5 degrees latitude, there are pyramids directly north and south of it. Uxmal in Mexico and Tikal in Guatemala are directly on this line. The same can be said for the underwater megalithic structures off the coast of Japan - 120 degrees further west. So why are they not on the precise points?

Carl Munck has worked out that earth energies are present at the longitude lines travelling north and south of 19.5 degrees. If we travel along these lines we find numerous sacred sites – notably pyramids. This image below shows how the pyramids at Tikal and Uxmal link directly with an underwater pyramid located in Rock Lake, Wisconsin where strange phenomena have been documented. An identical 'grid-band' has been shown to exist along the Giza plateau in Egypt, along which *all* the pyramids are located.

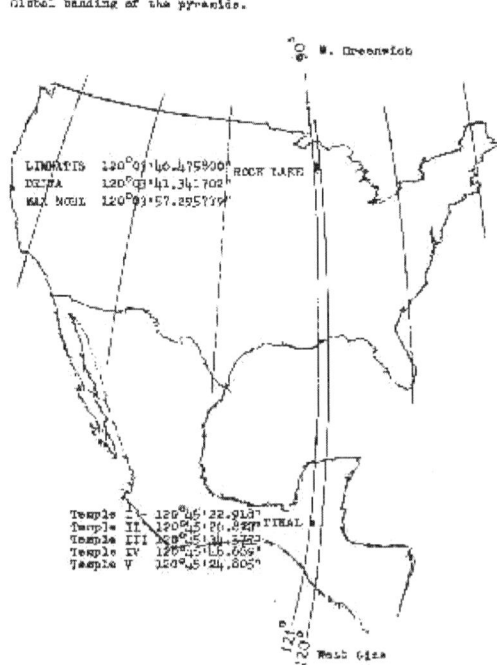

The grid-line of the Americas (Munck)

So the two sites that captured me on my travels have a harmonic link to each other. Since I had my 'triple visit' to Uxmal, I have had numerous dreams about being there in the distant past. As I mentioned in the 'Mexico Initiation' chapter, Tikal totally took me into its arms, but in a different way. Therefore, before I even knew about this aspect of the grid, I was somehow experiencing the effects in a particular way. The way in which I was called back to Uxmal on two extra occasions now becomes clear. I was being given a clue to the nature of its location on earth. As we have already seen, the north-south grid band echoes around the world at 120 degree intervals which represents the number 'three', or three points of the tetrahedron touching the surface of the sphere. At Tikal, I circled the Great Plaza three times. Hmmmm maybe?

THE ICOSA-DODECAHEDRON GRID

Ivan P Sanderson's discovery of the icosahedron grid ignited a world-wide interest and three Russians scientists: Nikolai Goncharov, a Muscovite historian, Vyacheslav Morozov, a construction engineer and Valery Makarov, an electronics specialist, took on the job of constructing a map that determined the earth's "Matrix of Cosmic Energy"(9). They super-imposed a dodecahedron (ten sided polygon with 20 points) onto the map and came up with this result:

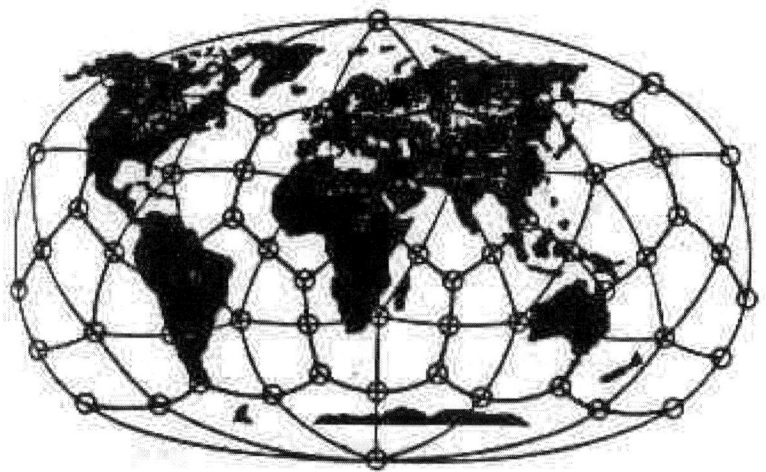

IcosaDodecahedron Grid (reprinted in 'Anti-Gravity and the World Grid')

The husband and wife team of William Becker, a Professor of Industrial Design and Bethe Hagans, a Professor of Anthropology, commented on this new discovery.

"These new lines and points, in conjunction with Sanderson's, now matched most of the Earth's seismic fracture zones and ocean ridge lines as well as outlined worldwide atmospheric highs and lows, paths of migratory animals, gravitational anomalies, and even the sites of ancient cities" (10) .

They improved this map with the help of the work of Chris Bird, who wrote an article on the planetary grid in the *New Age Journal* of May 1975. They had a meeting with him and they eventually made the grid compatible with all the Platonic Solids, by inserting a creation from Buckminster Fuller's work. Here is the technical version:

"We propose that the planetary grid map outlined by the Russian team Goncharov, Morozov and Makarov is essentially correct, with its overall organization anchored to the north and south axial poles and the Great Pyramid at Gizeh. The Russian map, however, lacks completeness, in our opinion, which can be accomplished by the overlaying of a complex, icosahedrally-derived, spherical polyhedron developed by R. Buckminster Fuller. In his book Synergetics 2, he called it the "Composite of Primary and Secondary Icosahedron Great Circle Sets." We have shortened that to Unified Vector Geometry (UVG) 120 sphere... We use the number 120 due to its easy comprehension as a spherical polyhedron with 120 identical triangles - all approximately 30, 60 and 90 in composition."

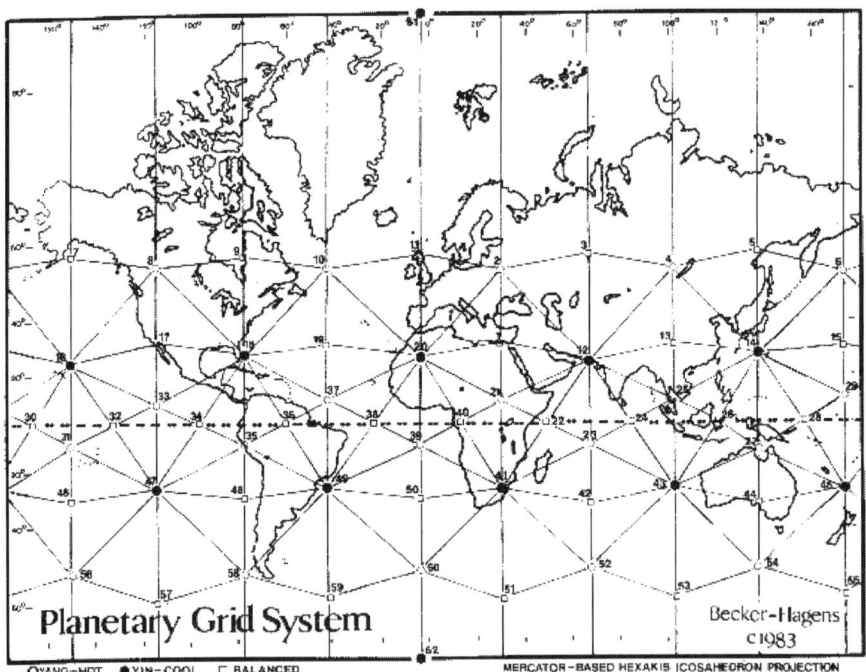

The Planetary Grid System shown [here] was inspired by an original article by Christopher Bird, "Planetary Grid," published in New Age Journal #5, May 1975, pp. 36-41. The hexakis icosahedron grid, coordinate calculations, and point classification system are the original research of Bethe Hagens and William S. Becker. These materials are distributed with permission of the authors by Conservative Technology Intl. in cooperation with Governors State University, Division of Intercultural Studies, University Park, Illinois

60466 312/534-5000 x2455. This map may be reproduced if they are distributed without charge and if acknowledgement is given to Governors State University (address included) and Mr. Bird.

METATRON & THE ANGELS

The importance of working with the planetary grid was mentioned by Grandmother Chandra at the conference when she said *"We must connect to the crystal grid that has been set up. Focus your intentions and join with it. The dodecahedron in sacred geometry will help with understanding the alignments* [of the grid]". The Dodecahedron is the closest resemblance in the Platonic solids sequence to the sphere and is represented by the Archangel Metatron, who is the final Angel before God. Chandra also said *"Metatron is working with us now"*, when talking about the grid. The planetary grid is often referred to as the Metatronic grid and this is where the rules of sacred geometry and the angelic realm merge.

'Lightwaves' by Jean Luc Bozzoli, showing a dodecahedron.

Chandra uses this angelic correspondence to enable us to relate to the grid in a simplified manner. The different angels and archangels seem to be a representation of varying types of energy that influence the energetic geometry of the earth. We have already seen how different vibrational frequencies create different geometric shapes within a sphere. Perhaps this is the true nature of angels and how they work with the earth. If we rearrange the letters of angel, we get 'angle', which signifies this mathematical connection.

'Archangel' encodes 'arc', 'arch' and 'angle' – all mathematical terms in geometry and architecture. There is a developing theory that the angels/angles are the instigators of the planetary grid and were the guiding, intelligent force behind its construction.

The dodecahedron was the 'mystery' Platonic solid in *The Timaeus*. It is often referred to as the most important geometric shape of the five. Again I would like to remind you that I firmly believe the combination of the Icosahedron and dodecahedron is the key shape that was once that 'mystery'. It is also interesting to discover that this shape contains *all the Platonic solids within its structure*. One can also see that Hawaii has reclaimed its prime placement on the grid map and it is clear how the landmasses seem to gel around many of the main points. In Australia, the node-point perfectly surrounds this energy upwelling. On the east coast of South America it is the same. The points of energy are easily discernable on this map. So we now have some background of how the grid was discovered and some insights into what type of energy we are dealing with here. This is where we now need to go out and reconnect to our lost energetic heritage.

WORKING WITH THE GRID

According to author and geomancer Michael Poynder, the three chakras above the head are a direct link to the grid around the earth. But what is really interesting is that the 9th chakra *is a dodecahedron with the other platonic solids floating around it*. Michael Poynder rediscovered this in his book *The Lost Magic of Christianity*. The higher chakras have been dowsed, felt by hand and seen psychically and clairvoyantly. Here is Poynder's description of these three chakras : (my emphasis)

8th Chakra – The chakra of the Higher Self, the spirit, **the Christ Consciousness**. *A sphere of blue-white light with hundreds of points in all directions. First manifested as a three to twelve-pointed star, and the eight-pointed star of the Knights Templar. Out of this chakra, healing through pure love is possible.*

9th Chakra – A golden, oval ring, with the longer sides wider than the shorter sides. Inside the ring, three-dimensional forms appear, one at a time, representing the five elements. **The form pictures within the ring represents spiritual power, the binding element, the essence, the dodecahedron**. *Around the ring the other elements are drawn: earth, water, air, fire. According to some, this chakra is the archetype of the self. Psychics can see a damaged ring in case of illness or ailment. Spiritual healers can apply healing here. The five Platonic solids (tetrahedron, octahedron, icosahedron, cube and dodecahedron) represent the building blocks of reality and the life force.*

10th Chakra *– Round this sphere, blue cord-like shapes are moving in a jerky way. This chakra is considered the archetype of the Earth and suggests our unbreakable connection with Mother Earth and our responsibility for 'Her', for Gaia – the Goddess.*

It can now be seen that these chakras are a connector to the grid, through Christ Consciousness, the Platonic solids and a love for mother earth. These factors represent a trinity of knowledge that are useful in earth grid work. To successfully anchor the grid energy into ourselves and the earth, we must be fully conscious and have strong intentions to do so. Calling on Metatron to assist in the process can also help, as will visualising what you want the outcome to be. Remember – we are the ones now responsible for our own evolution. To believe that 'everything is going to be alright' is not on the agenda. We are part of the earth and the earth is part of us. We are planetary consciousness and we work for each other. Now it is unquestionably our turn to get busy.

Simon Peter Fuller later told me that to meditate *before* you go to the chosen location is useful and when you have finished, leave the site immediately, maintaining focus. Don't linger and start smoking cigarettes. I was up on Glastonbury Tor recently and a group from America were carrying out what they called "important grid work". The group leader left an empty diet-coke can and used cigarette butts for us onlookers to clear up. This does not sound like they are respecting the energies.

Michael Helus believes that planetary grid harmonics can, and will be manipulated if we do not develop a responsible stewardship for this profound and powerful resource (10). He suggests that the severe changes in weather patterns are not natural because the grid is no longer fixed to the north and south poles. This is why so many communities around the world are meeting at the relevant sites to become maintenance workers and intuit their way to helping Gaia. As we have already discussed, the main sacred sites are built upon this grid and have kept the planetary energies in balance for millennia, but things are changing dramatically in our solar system that is over-burdening the grid to extremes, but many are starting to become attuned to Gaia's needs and have heard the call from the Mother.

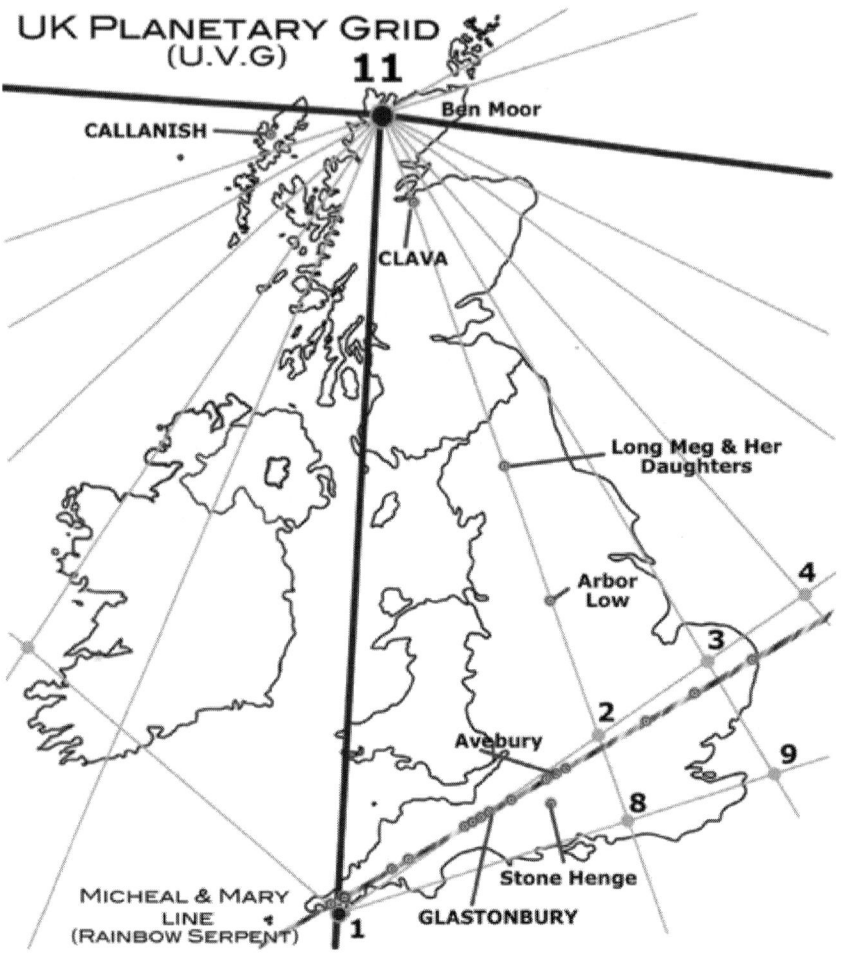

This map shows the basics of the British part of the grid and pinpoints many ancient sacred sites, notably Glastonbury and Avebury. The reason this alignment stands out, is that it corresponds with the St.Michael ley-line, as discovered by John Michell in the 1970's. On the above map it is the line that goes north east from the tip of Cornwall to the East Anglian coast, and has an almost identical path to this geometry of the planetary grid. It was later found by Hamish Miller and Paul Broadhurst in their book *The Sun and the Serpent* that powerful feminine and masculine energy lines weave around this straight-line alignment.

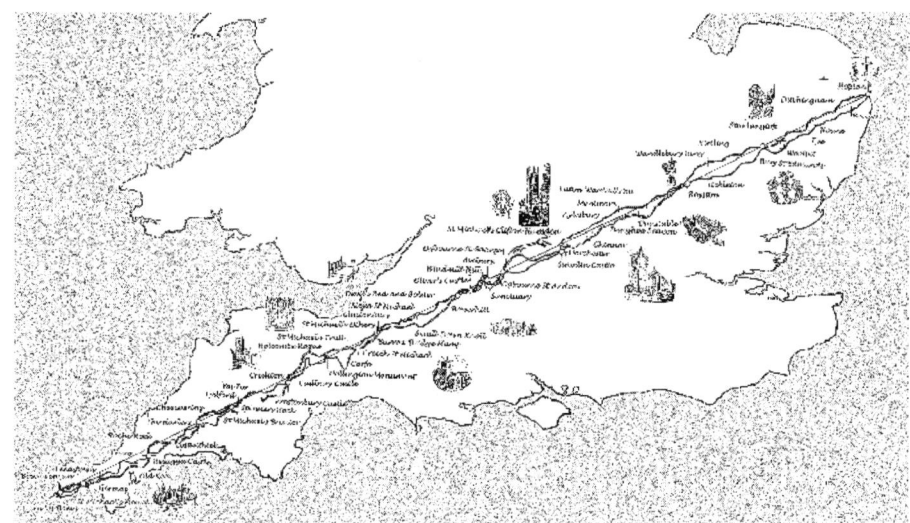

The Michael & Mary energy currents

But, it does not end there; this energy current travels around the whole planet and through specific sacred sites and cities. The Aborigines call it the 'Rainbow Serpent' and authors such as Robert Coon and Simon Peter Fuller have been involved with activating certain points on it. These are related to the chakra points of the planet, with a mutable third-eye chakra point that has been located in Jerusalem for the last two thousand years. Simon Peter Fuller and Robert Coon are fully aware of the nature of grid-work and have been travelling Gaia on a bizarre but fruitful mission; the maintenance and activation of the planetary chakra system.

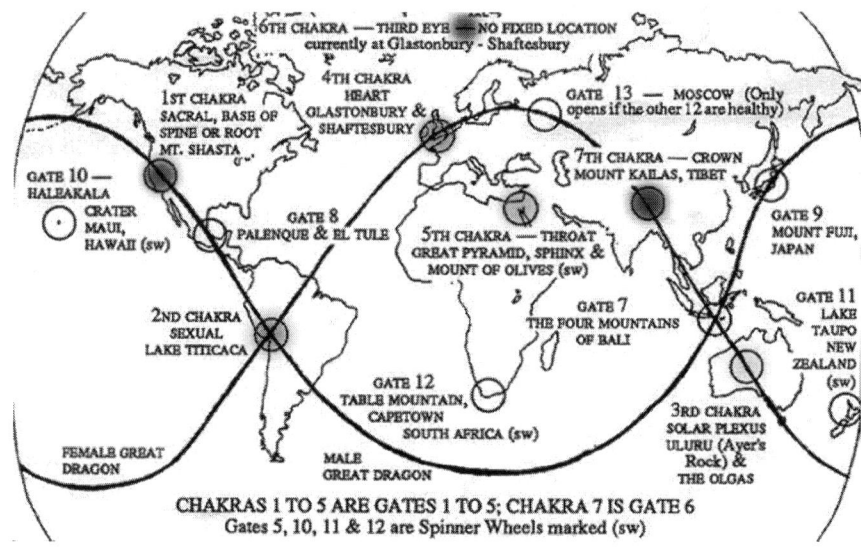

A series of synchronicities led to a group of grid-workers I am involved with being sent hundred of crystals from some Aborigine elders, with the instructions to place them along the British segment of the Rainbow Serpent and to *'activate the British dreamtime'* (11). According to them, part of it was not functioning properly and needed attention. I felt slightly bemused by what was involved. We had to get to as many of the sites as possible before the upcoming deadline of November 8th 2003 – also known as Harmonic Concordance. The journey took fifty of us all over the British Isles, with the final placement at Glastonbury Tor, the heart chakra of the planet, on the evening of Harmonic Concordance – November 8th 2003. The mutable third-eye chakra has now been anchored at the site of the 'New Jerusalem' – Glastonbury.

THE HUMAN EFFECT

3,300 ancient sacred sites have been discovered on the Becker/Hagens grid so far and there are probably many more. So what we have here is an ancient wisdom connecting with modern-day knowledge. The builders from the past *knew* we needed their knowledge today, so that we could have a smooth ride through to the next dimension, on a planet that is an integral part of our own body. As the earth geometrically reconfigures herself, we must keep up with the 'maintenance' work to keep her running smoothly. The children know this and this is one of their main teachings. The Hopi also knew about the 'shift of the ages'. In one of their prophecies they describe the earth's surface as being similar to the back of a spotted fawn. As the fawn symbolically grows, the spots move and change number. Similarly, every time the earth enters a new vibrational frequency, her power centres also change to a new configuration, interconnected by a more complex sacred geometry.

We now know exactly where the grid is across our planet. But us humans, we also influence this grid so some degree. The movement of civilisations across continents influences the grid in profound ways. The energy of thousands of people in one location over centuries increases energy in the planetary grid system. Our electro-magnetic energy is directly linked to the earth's electro-magnetic energy. The grid is therefore constructed and altered as to where *we choose to position ourselves within it (12)*. This helps explain why many sacred sites are not directly on the grid. David Wilcock addressed another reason that the sacred sites are not all on 'node-points'. He believes they are placed at complex intersections or *stress points* between the grid and other forces on the planet. The earthworks and stone circles were *"constructed where they needed to be built."*

"These separate points had structures built around them in order to make them useful for the purposes of healing and/or planetary balancing. These were the two primary functions………. So therefore, in going about this in the most complete way possible, we can see that without having done this to such

*amazing fastidiousness and precision, then the system itself would have been incomplete. In many cases, it was the **structure itself** that was of highest import, not as much the way that it was built, which was to encode its grid latitude and longitude position.*

The structure itself was necessary to be built along certain lines in order to regularize the energy flows therein. And thus, you do see a great many stone circles, or earth circles, as in certain cases, the circle is by far the most adequate energy regularizer for grid fluctuations. Remember that these grid fluctuations are caused largely by the consciousness of the planet's inhabitants" (ibid).

So there we have it. The history of the grid up to the present day and how the children (and us) can work with it to maintain the energetic balance on our home planet. Use of the grid is an important factor with the psychic children. They have learnt how to tune in to the frequency that the grid resonates at and can use it for telepathy, healing and grid-balancing. This is the same way that Australian Aborigines explain the 'song lines'. They once used the paths of the grid to communicate over vast distances. We have come full-circle and the children have helped us remember that it was our own relatives that were involved in the building of many of these ancient sacred sites. It is no wonder that we are 'needing' to get out to these sites with deep fascination and interest.

4. NUTRITION FOR THE NEW HUMAN

I do not mean to get parents alarmed by the information I am about to share with you in this chapter. I am simply presenting what the companies that provide all these products already know. The chemical soup that our children are ingesting needs another look, because the sheer amount of toxins we now have to deal with is at a record high. There are alternatives to every single chemical-laden product that is mentioned in this chapter. When it comes to food, this is where you need to constantly read the labels. I am always scanning the ingredients list of foods aimed at children in supermarkets and even health-food shops and I am increasingly alarmed at what I am seeing. This research is outlined in the rest of this chapter.

THE DANGERS OF RITALIN

Children are often diagnosed with attention deficit disorder (ADD), attention deficit hyperactivity disorder (ADHD) and oppositional defiant disorder (ODD) [1]. Doctors and even teachers recommend the psycho-stimulant drug Ritalin to deal with these 'problem children'. It is estimated that more than six million American children take psychotropic medication for ADHD, depression and other psychological maladies [2]. A study for the Office of National Statistics in Britain, discovered that about three percent of five- to 10- year-olds and almost four percent of 11- to 15-year-olds have 'conduct disorders' [1]. Psychologists and child specialists question the use of such labels, saying that the problem often lies with the adults who are looking after them. The parents and teachers abdicate responsibility, which leads to the prescription of drugs such as Dexedrine, Cylert, Prozak, Paxil, Tofranil and Norpamin.

In 1998, the US National Institute of Mental Health held a conference focusing on the diagnosis and treatment of ADD and ADHD [2]. It was hoped a clear and concise evaluation would be reached by consensus. But this is not what happened. The panel basically said that they were not sure if either ADD or ADHD were "valid" conditions. There were no provable reasons for ever using the ADD and ADHD labels. They also found that ADHD has nothing to do with impaired brain function. What came from the conference were more questions than answers. If these conditions cannot be properly diagnosed it clearly suggests that they may not even exist. Why then are our children being poisoned with Ritalin and other drugs?

The children who take Ritalin soon lose many of the positive traits associated with the psychic children; such as intuition, telepathy and their warrior personality. Our children were given these qualities for good reasons. What appears to be slow learning and lack of attention are enough to get children on Ritalin, but it has become apparent that they actually get bored very easily by what they are being taught. The school syllabus does not do justice for the type of super human being we are dealing with here. These children need time and space to explore their intelligence and psychic gifts. Teachers often think they are 'playing up', but this is simply because they learn *too fast* for the schools they are in. It is the system that needs to change, not our children. These children are here to *change* the systems, not to conform. This is why many of the Indigos have such integrity, focus and power. They are the pioneers of the new type of human being and a new way of living in society. The people who produce and enforce the use of Ritalin know this.

Many of the children diagnosed with these conditions are, as we have seen, incredibly intelligent. Their IQ's are often as high as 130; 100 is the average. Many have IQ's in the genius range of 160. Recently I found out that the tests they once used for testing if a child was a genius is exactly the same test they now use to diagnose ADD and ADHD! So it looks like the Doctors actually do know that the population of geniuses is on the increase. The psychic children are living proof of the human potential. This leads me to ask the question; why are these children put on Ritalin? And is there a valid reason to pump them full of dangerous pharmaceuticals?

Doctor's get commission every time they prescribe a drug from a certain company. It has become their livelihood. Doctor's do not get taught nutrition or herbal medicine in their seven years of training, they get taught how to prescribe drugs produced by the pharmaceutical industry. They are also discouraged from studying such subjects and therefore not able use them on their patients. Doctor's colleges are funded by the same companies that produce and manufacture the drugs. Incentives for Doctors to prescribe certain drugs has become high. Each drug company has representatives trying to convince them that their drug is the best. Although officially it is not bribery, drug companies spend an average of $13,000 per year on each doctor in the USA (3). This adds up to $8 billion per year. The money goes on drug samples, ticket to sports events, dinners and holidays to beach or ski resorts. Drug companies employ 70,000 sales representatives, which equates to one representative for every nine doctors (3). A recent analysis of sixteen various studies demonstrated that doctors were more likely to perform "non-rational prescribing". This is where the doctor prescribes drugs that are more expensive and is less effective than what the patient requires (ibid).

There are well known natural alternatives for many serious conditions, but there is no profit because nature provides it and so it cannot be patented. Doctors are also the third leading cause of death in the US (4). Also, on average there are 106,000 deaths per year from *"non-error, adverse effects of medications"*. These are basically the *correct* drugs for conditions in the *correct* dosage.

The next quote is from a book called *How To Raise a Healthy Child.....in Spite of Your Doctor,* by Robert Mendelsohn MD. This abridged entry (with Mendleson's comments in brackets) was supplied by the producers of Ritalin, Ciba-Geigy. Note how they are not even sure how Ritalin works or how it affects the nervous system.

"Nervousness and insomnia are the most common adverse reactions but are usually controlled by reducing dosage and omitting the drug in the afternoon or evening. Other reactions include hypersensitivity (including skin rash), urticaria (swollen, itching patches of skin), fever, arthralgia, exfoliative dermatitis (scaly patches of skin), erythema multiforme (an acute inflammatory skin disease), with histopathological findings of necrotizing vasculitis (destruction of the blood vessels), and thrombocytopenic purpurea (a serious blood clotting disorder), anorexia; nausea; dizziness; palipatations; headache; dyskinesia (impairment of voluntary muscle movement), drowsiness; blood pressure and pulse changes, both up and down; tachycardia (rapid heartbeat), angina (spasmodic attacks of intense heart pain); cardiac arrhythmia (irregular heartbeat); abdominal pain, weight loss during prolonged therapy."

There have been rare reports of Tourette's syndrome as another side-effect. Toxic psychosis has been reported in patients taking this drug; leukopenia (reduction in white blood cells) and/or anemia; a few instances of scalp hair loss. In children, loss of appetite, abdominal pain, weight loss during prolonged therapy, insomnia, and tachycardia may occur more frequently; however, any of the other adverse reactions listed above may also occur (5).

So if the Doctors know all this, and the drug companies, by law have to tell them, how can they possibly prescribe such a drug? It is clear that Ritalin is not the answer. So lets look at what to avoid, to help with ADD, ADHD and ODD. Then we can delve in to what changes need to be made in the diet of our children.

AVOIDANCE TACTICS

Nutrition is the key in all of the conditions mentioned. But first of all we need to be fully aware of what *not* to ingest. Avoiding food additives is vital. The sheer amount of toxins, chemicals and e-numbers in our food at this moment in time bewilders me. There are over 540 permitted chemical additives in food. We know little about the 'cocktail' effect of these pesticides, artificial colourings, flavourings and preservatives. Research is currently underway regarding this and we now have up to date information at our fingertips to enable the first line of defence to be in place. *The Guardian* produced a three-part expose of the toxic overload we have to deal with called *Chemical World*. It can be viewed at the website: guardian.co.uk/chemicalworld. It is well worth having your own print out of all three parts.

Studies have shown that children's behaviour is directly affected by artificial colourings, sweeteners and flavourings. Fizzy drinks, sweets and crisps are the main culprits and there are now organic and chemical free alternatives in supermarkets and health food shops. Here are the main additives to avoid:

Flavour Enhancers: Monosodium glutamate (E621); disodium 5-ribonucleotide (E635); **Artificial Sweetners**: Sodium benzoate (E211); Sulphur dioxide (E220); aspartame; acesulfame K. **Colourings:** Yellow (E104), Brilliant blue (E113), sunset yellow (E110), carmoisine (E122), ponceau 4R (E124), allura red AC (E129) and indigo (!) carmine (E132).

Both sodium benzoate (E211) and carmoisine (E122) are directly linked to hyperactivity and can lead to eczema, asthma, urticaria (skin rash) or rhinitis [6]. Many of these additives have been banned in the US, Denmark and Sweden, but have been passed as safe in the UK. Also note that terms such as 'flavourings' or 'colourings' are usually chemical compounds that are best avoided. If it says 'cheese flavoured', it means it has cheese in it. If it says 'cheese flavour' it does not. Look at food labels and learn the chemical names. Knowledge is vital to create good health.

Flavoured crisps are a chemical cocktail. Each pack has roughly one gram of **salt**. Half the recommended daily dose for a six-year-old [7]. One third of a pack is pure fat. Researchers in Sweden discovered **acrylamide** in cooked fatty products including crisps. It is known to cause cancer in animals and could possibly do the same for humans. Crisps might also contain **Monosodium glutomate** which is linked to serious health disorders (see next section). *Disodium 5'-ribonucleotide,* another flavour enhancer that is linked to skin rashes and has been banned in Australia. *Aspartame,* an artificial sweetener is surprisingly in many brands of crisps. This has also been linked to many serious health disorders (next section).

Nick Giovannelli, of the Hyperactive Children's support Group, believes that about 5% of children are 'extra-sensitive' to additives. He explains that additives clog up neurotransmitters that have been shown to lead to difficult and bizarre behavior in children. He also noted how additives prevent the absorption of the mineral zinc, a deficiency of which has been related to hyperactivity [8]. Zinc is believed to regulate the supply of the brain chemical dopamine, which improves concentration and lessens impulsiveness.

An experiment was shown on ITV's *Tonight with Trevor McDonald* on 28th April 2003 that summed up what nutritionists have known for years. One set of twin boys were put on different diets for two weeks. While Christopher continued feasting on chocolate, crisps and fizzy drinks full of E numbers, Michael was eating fresh fruit, vegetables, nuts and cereals. Before the experiment, they had IQ tests and the results were identical. Two weeks later and Michael was beating his brother in IQ and concentration tests by 15%. Michael's behavior changed radically. He became calmer, more talkative, developed a sense of humour and 'did as he was told' more frequently. When the E number ban was introduced to the twins' class at Dingle School in Crewe, 60% of parents reported improvement in their children's behaviour, sleep patterns and ability to co-operate.

A similar experiment took place at Ysgol Deganwy Primary School in Conwy, Wales that showed similar results. This sort of scheme is vital to bring awareness of the dangers of 'junk food' and E numbers. Please talk to your school about setting up similar schemes. Every single school that has performed these experiments has shown a dramatic decrease in bad behavior and an increase in concentration. The *Soil Association* (soilassociation.org) is working with *Food for Life* (foodforlife.org) to get organic local food into schools. School cook, Jeanette Orrey pioneered getting mostly fresh organic meals at St. Peter's Primary School in East Bridgford, Nottinghamshire. To get an action pack check out the websites mentioned. Also check out eostreorganics.co.uk and localfoodworks.org. Many schools now ban sweets and crisps and run a Healthy Snack Policy. To find out how to set up a school based fruit shop, download the form from: food.gov.uk/multimedia/pdfs/fruittuckwales.

HYDROGENATED FATS

Hydrogenated fats and **Trans-fats** are in processed foods such as crisps, cakes, biscuits, ready-meals, pies, pasties, chips, batter, sausages, vegetarian sausages and cheap margarine. These are vegetable oils that are 'hardened' by a process of pumping hydrogen into the oil, which creates saturated and the more dangerous trans-fats. Trans-fats have got scientists concerned, who believe that these are more damaging than saturated fats. This type of fat is not recognized by the body and is linked to high cholesterol and heart disease (9). It also stops the essential fats (Omega 3 and 6) getting properly absorbed by the body. On labels look out for "hydrogenated" or "partially hydrogenated" fat/oils. A small reduction of their intake will help, because this type of fat is widespread in basic food products. Margarine is the main culprit, so go for the healthy options from whole food stores. They usually stock various brands.

EXCITOTOXINS

Monosodium Glutamate, Aspartame and **Hydrolysed Vegetable Protein** all fall under the same umbrella of 'Exciototoxins'. These compounds react with specialized receptors in the brain in such a way as to lead to the destruction of various neurons. They do not have a dramatic effect, but slowly build up and gradually weaken the body over time. Exciototoxins have been linked to learning disorders in children (10). They also play a critical role in the development of other neurological disorders, including migraines, seizures, infections, abnormal neural development, endocrine disorders, neuropsychicatric disorders, AIDS, dementia, episodic violence, specific types of obesity, lyme borreliosis, hepatic encephalopathy, and especially the neurodegenerative diseases such as amyotrophic lateral sclerosis (ALS), Parkinson's disease, Alzheimer's disease, Huntington's disease and olivopontocerebellar degeneration. (11). Exciototoxins are also linked to DNA damage. Cellular proteins and mitochondrial DNA are the most affected. DNA is our last line of defence in any health matter. If our DNA gets affected, then everything gets affected.

Monosodium glutamate (E621) and **Disodium 5'-ribonucleotide** (E635) are banned from foods for children under the age of three, but that does not stop them getting in foods that young children still eat. The neurotoxin Monosodium Glutamate (MSG) has been campaigned against for years. It is a white powder well know in Chinese cooking, but has been linked to many of the conditions mentioned above. MSG is found in many processed products and is used as an alternative to salt. Crisps, stock cubes, ready meals and a host of cheap processed food are the culprits. Remember to read the labels.

Aspartame is an artificial sweetener found in carbonated drinks, crisps and many processed 'diet' foods. Also known as NutraSweet, Equal, Spoonful and Equal-Measure, aspartame is, by far, the most dangerous substance that is put in foods. Aspartame accounts for over 75 percent of the adverse reactions to food additives reported to the US Food and Drug Administration (FDA). These reactions include seizures and even death. In the report there are 90 different documented symptoms (12). These include: Headaches/migraines, dizziness, seizures, nausea, numbness, muscle spasms, weight gain, rashes, depression, fatigue, irritability, tachycardia, insomnia, vision problems, hearing loss, heart palpitations, breathing difficulties, anxiety attacks, slurred speech, loss of taste, tinnitus, vertigo, memory loss, and joint pain.

Chronic illnesses can be triggered or worsened by ingesting aspartame: (13) - Brain tumours, multiple sclerosis, epilepsy, chronic fatigue syndrome, parkinson's disease, alzheimer's, mental retardation, lymphoma, birth defects, fibromyalgia, and diabetes. There is no compelling scientific evidence that it *causes* these conditions, but the reports keep coming in from people who have ingested it and recent this research suggests there is a definite link (14).

SUGAR BLUES

Sugar offers no useful nutrition; it actually strips nutrients from the body; contributes to excessive weight gain and is linked to tooth decay; it stresses the pancreas and can lead to diabetes and hypoglyceamia (low blood sugar). People who cannot handle sugar have symptoms such as: fatigue, nervousness, depression, apprehension, craving for sweets, inability to handle alcohol, inability to concentrate, allergies and low blood pressure (15).

Mary Ann Block, D.O.,P.A., author of *No More Ritalin,* believes that many of the symptoms linked to ADD and ADHD could be due to hypoglycemia. She states that this condition *"is the most significant underlying problem I find in children who exhibit behavioural problems"*. She lists the behavioural symptoms of hypoglycemia as *"the child who is agitated or irritable when he or she wakes up in the morning, or before meals, and then is better after eating: and the child with the Jekyll and Hyde behaviour, who is sweet and fine one minute, and then for no apparent reason, is agitated, angry, and irritable the next".* Changing simple things in the diet are the key. *"Make sure the child never gets hungry, and eliminate refined carbohydrates, such as candy, cakes, pies, and soft drinks".* Do not make children wait for dinner if they are hungry. Give them a healthy snack.

Sugar has also been scientifically linked to hyperactivity. Some studies do not show this link, but when Yale University researchers gave white sugar to children and compared their blood adrenaline levels before and after, they found the levels were ten times higher (16). Adrenaline is a heart pumping chemical produced by the adrenal glands that prepares you for dangerous situations. They also found that the children were anxious, irritable and had difficulty concentrating after consuming sugar (17). Be aware that it is sugar that is the major cause of childhood obesity, not fat. It gets stored and if it is not used up in exercise it turns into fat.

Clinical research with hyperactive and psychotic children, as well as those with brain injuries and learning disabilities, has shown: *"An abnormally high family history of diabetes-that is, parents and grandparents who cannot handle sugar; an abnormally high incidence of low blood glucose, or functional hypoglycemia in the children themselves, which indicates that their systems cannot handle sugar; dependence on a high level of sugar in the diets of the very children who cannot handle it. Inquiry into the dietary history of patients diagnosed as schizophrenic reveals the diet of their choice is rich in sweets, candy, cakes, coffee, caffeinated beverages, and foods prepared with sugar. These foods, which stimulate the adrenals, should be eliminated or severely restricted"* (18).

Refined sugar is the worst because when it goes into our bloodstream, it is not in its whole form, therefore the nutrients that are missing from the refining process (mollasses) are taken from the reserves in the body. It is an anti-nutrient and should be avoided wherever possible. Sugar and white (refined) flour bypasses the digestive process because the fibre has been stripped from the food. The small molecules then can easily enter directly in to the bloodstream in the small intestine. The body works flat out to remove the surplus from the bloodstream leaving the bloodstream with very low sugar levels, and the person feeling tired and lacking in energy. These fluctuating blood sugar levels can put the body under too much stress and the system controlling blood sugar starts to break down. The result can be diabetes.

SUGAR ALTERNATIVES

In 1991, the FDA banned the importation of **Stevia**. The powder of the leaf has been used for hundreds of years as an alternative sweetener. It is used widely in Japan with no adverse effects. Scientists involved in reviewing stevia have declared it to be safe for human consumption - something that has been well known in many parts of the world where it is not banned. Everyone that I have spoken with in regards to this issue believes that stevia was banned to keep the product from taking hold in the US and cutting into sales of aspartame (19).

Xylitol is another alternative sweetener that also has incredible health benefits. Extracted from birch bark, recent research has shown that it has many healing effects, especially for those sensitive to sugar. Although it looks and tastes very similar to sugar, Xylitol does not function in the same way. Where sugar has a negative effect on the body, Xylitol heals and repairs. It helps build a strong immune system, protects against degenerative diseases and even has anti-ageing benefits (20). It is an antimicrobial, therefore preventing the growth of bacteria. It is alkaline, whereas sugar is acidic. An alkaline digestive system is vital for good health. Sugar and related substances (sucrose, glucose, fructose, maltose, lactose etc) feed dangerous bacteria and fungi in the body that can lead to conditions such as candida.

The most important aspect of Xylitol is how it stops sugar and carbohydrate cravings. Its use cannot lead to obesity because it is a slow releasing carbohydrate. Over 1,500 scientific studies have found that the more you use Xylitol, sugar cravings become less and less. It also reduces insulin levels, so it is safe for diabetics. It is the perfect alternative to sugar, especially for children who have a 'sweet tooth'.

PESTICIDES

Pesticide is a chemical that 'kills' pests, and this negative energy is found in most non-organic fruit, vegetables, grains and oils. In April 2004, a comprehensive review of pesticides was produced by the Ontario College of Family Physicians highlighting the dangers of over exposure (21). It found consistent links to several cancers, including brain, kidney, prostate and pancreatic, and leukaemia, as well as reproductive problems and neurological disorders. It made it clear that *"children are particularly vulnerable"* (22).

Meat contains pesticides, hormones and chemicals and has a 'death' energy associated with it. When an animal gets killed, it knows its death is coming. It gets an adrenaline rush which then stays in the meat, and is then consumed. Children who eat poor-quality red meats can be aggressive and/or emotionally stressed. This is partly due to the fatty acid arachidonate, which promotes mental and physical inflammation, and therefore aggression. As this internal aggression-based stress accumulates, intoxicants become more attractive later in life for their (temporary) relaxing value (ibid).

Bread may also contain pesticides. A recent investigation by the governments pesticide residue committee found that 78% of wholemeal breads found in supermarkets contain the pesticide chlormequat (23). Wholemeal bread also has more fat than white bread, and the fats that are generally used are not easily recognized by the body. White bread is made with refined flour and works with the body just like sugar. It bypasses the digestive tract to give a boost of energy, but lacks the nutrients and 'wholeness' for proper absorption. Wheat allergies are also an ongoing problem. Many children react to the gluten in wheat and develop an allergy or intolerance later in life. Tiredness and irritability are the symptoms associated with this allergy.

THERE'S SOMETHING IN THE WATER

Chemicals and additives in our water supply have been under the spotlight recently. **Fluoride** is the main concern. The silicofluorides used in household water supplies are toxic waste from the phosphate fertiliser companies. They contain dangerous amounts of lead, arsenic, mercury, beryllium and radionuclides (24). They are all registered as a 'part 2 poison' under the 1972 Poisons Act and are in violation of the 'Offences Against the Persons Act 1861', which forbids the administration of any poisonous substance (ibid).

The UK Government has recently passed a Water Bill, making it illegal for water companies to 'not' add fluoride to drinking water. How this got through un-noticed remains a mystery. Fortunately, the National Pure Water association (NPWA) are on the case. They are running an ongoing campaign to stop compulsory water fluoridation in our water supplies. Check out: npwa.freeserve.co.uk to get involved. There is a sense of urgency regarding the safety of our water, and if we, as individuals do not do something about it, we can say goodbye to our drinking water for good.

The dangers of fluoride are quite spectacular. Dentists still believe it strengthens our teeth, but this is not exactly true. It actually causes dental fluorosis, which is the mottling and pitting of teeth and has been known about since 1936 (25). It also causes skeletal fluorosis, weakened bone structure and is linked to lowered IQs in children. Fluoride displaces the mineral iodine which leads to hypothyrodism (sluggish metabolism). It increases the risk of bone cancer in adolescent males; it can cause osteoporosis and has led to hip fractures.

Fluoride has also been found to interfere with the pineal gland and its release of melatonin. The pineal gland is currently becoming activated in humanity, so there is a whiff of conspiracy suggested here. The pineal gland produces melatonin that is linked to psychic activity, maintaining the strength of the immune system, preventing cancer and regulating the onset of puberty. Early puberty has been shown to exist in areas where there is fluoride in the water (26).

As mentioned earlier, fluoride is linked to a lower IQ in children. This has been well documented in a report by researchers in China. In one community where there were high fluoride levels, the average IQ was 98. In the other tested area where the fluoride levels were low, the average was 105 (ibid). An IQ shift of 7 points in an entire population has large population-wide implications, as well as impacting individual members, therefore these results deserve close attention regarding what this mass medication is doing to our children's brains. Babies fed milk formula made with tap water receive 50-100 times more fluoride than those that are breast-fed (27). To find out if your water has fluoride in it, call up your local water company. Legally, they have to tell you. If it is, check out: npwa.freeserve.co.uk for alternatives.

BABYCARE PRODUCTS

When choosing babycare products, 'Best ever softness', 'hypoallergenic' and 'dermatologically tested' do not quite mean what they appear to. Your average babycare product contains a cocktail of chemicals that are disguised as parfum, preservatives and colours. Look at labels on baby-wipes, shampoo, nappy cream, bubble-bath's, talcum powder and anything else going on your child's skin. A baby's skin and blood brain barrier is very thin compared to adults, so more chemicals can build up and lead to serious health disorders. Warm water is enough to clean a baby, so why do we need to chance it with these products?

Sodium Laurel Sulphate is found in products such as Johnson's 'No More Tears' baby shampoo, Avent's 'Baby Body and Hair Wash' and Boots' 'Sleep Baby and Child Bath Bubbles'. It is a commercial detergent and is safe in very low doses if washed off the skin, but can trigger eczema if in prolonged contact with the skin in high concentrations (28).

Talcum powder can irritate the lungs and cause breathing problems if inhaled in large quantities. Past studies have shown a link between long-term genital use and ovarian cancer, but talc is not considered to be toxic in any way by the regulatory bodies (ibid).

Parfum can contain any of 200 different synthetic chemicals, so look out for that on labels.

Propylene glycol is in numerous baby products and has been linked to depressing the central nervous system (the nerves that make up the brain and spinal cord). It is an irritant and easily absorbed by the skin (especially babies' skin) and has been linked to fatalities in premature babies (29).

Parabens are also worth watching out for. This family of compounds are mainly used as preservatives and are skin and eye irritants. They have also been found to mimic the female hormone oestrogen and have even been found in human breast tumors. This has led to suggestions that parabens are linked to breast cancer (ibid).

To find out where to get non-toxic baby products, go to newhuman.co.uk

PREGNANCY

Vitamin A or **Retinol** is found in many cosmetic products and should be avoided. Too much of this in the bloodstream can interfere with the development of the foetus and can lead to malformations. Vitamin A supplements should also be left well alone (unless otherwise advised).

Suncreams can also be toxic. Dr.Martin Schlumpf, an environmental toxicoligist from the University of Zurich has been studying the ingredients of suncreams. Nine out of ten compounds in the creams mimicked oestrogen (see above) and some were found that were related to camphor (30).

Birch and Wintergreen essential oils contain the chemical methyl salicylate and are best avoided. Women with a record of early miscarriage may want to avoid clary sage.

Very hot baths are not a good idea. They can cause a number of problems.

WATER BIRTHING

Water birthing has been used by thousands of mothers as a more peaceful way to bring a child into existence. It gives the child a smooth entrance from the water-reality they have been in for nine months in the mother's womb, into the world we know and love. But when dolphins get involved it brings another dimension to giving birth. Let's look at the traditional method first. Childbirth can be a painful experience for all involved. Babies who are born into a brightly lit, claustrophobic atmosphere with forceps pulling them away from the peace of the Mothers womb, can often leave the baby traumatised. Then gasping for their first breath with the cutting of the umbilical cord seconds later is the second major shock, and all this before it has a chance to connect with the Mother.

A practice called 'rebirthing' was created by Leanord Orr, so that adults can be regressed back to birth to re-live the traumatic experience. It was quickly discovered that a 'bad' birth could have consequences that echoed through their whole life. Rebirthing is now very popular and psychologists sometimes refer their patients to rebirthers because there is nothing more they can do for them. If you think about it, birth is the most potent experience in life and if it is not facilitated properly, the consequences can be devastating.

The answer seems to lie in the world's most abundant natural resource – water. The benefits of spending time in water during pregnancy and for the actual birth far outstrip those of a traditional hospital birth. Water relieves the strain of gravity on the body during pregnancy and lessens the nerve impulses to the brain. It also has a calming effect on the mind. Scientific studies have shown that the reduction of pain is so significant that there is often no need for epidurals, drugs, or forceps.

Thousands of underwater births have been carried out in France. When they started doing this, they had all the emergency supplies and medical instruments laid out on a table nearby. But they never had any problems for a long time. In fact, for the entire 20,000 births they did not have one single complication. It seems that floating in water is the ultimately natural way to give birth. There are legends and stories of water birthing from the Maoris, the

American Indians near Panama, the Aborigines and the ancient Greeks. It is also said that some priests in ancient Egypt were born in water.

BIRTH WITH DOLPHINS

Igor Charkovsky, a Russian male mid-wife/shaman has assisted in over several thousand underwater births, but in 1979 he began experiments with dolphins and children. His daughter, one of the first modern water-birthers, was in her late twenties when the following incident happened. Charkovsky and his team had taken a woman to the Black Sea in Israel for an underwater birth. In two feet of water, preparing for the birth, suddenly three dolphins approached, pushed everyone out of the way and took over. They scanned the length of her body (with sonar?), which somehow relaxed the mother and child and gave birth with no pain or fear. Apparently all the human midwives were pretty shocked though. This opened up the new practice of 'Dolphin midwifery' that may sound strange, but fits in with the new breed of super-children that are currently coming in to existence.

For some reason, dolphins are attracted to pregnant women and young children and as most people are aware, the dolphins can also help heal people with mental and psychological problems. But the children, who are being born with the aid of dolphins, at least with the cases documented in Russia, are extraordinary children. Most of the have IQ's of over 150 (genius range again), plus extremely stable emotional bodies and strong physical bodies. They are superior in one way or another.

Charkovsky has shown videos that document these babies and children up to age three, sleeping on the bottom of swimming pools. They even come up for air whilst still asleep and turn their heads over the surface of the water, take a breath, then go back to the bottom. It is as though this is their natural home. Some people call them 'Homodolphinus', because they seem to be a blend of human and dolphin. Water is becoming their natural environment, plus they are also super-intelligent.

There is ample evidence that humans once had a much more intrinsic connection with water. Charkovsky believes that mans close affinity with aquatic animals can be explained by our common origins in water in our mammalian history. In the book *The Aquatic Ape*, Elaine Morgan gives a fascinating account of the aquatic theory of evolution. According to Morgan, our aquatic affinity goes back millions of years to the Pliocene age, when our ape ancestors lived a semi-aquatic life on the coastline to escape the extreme heat that occurred due to climatic change. By wading in the sea, our ancestors began to walk upright and lost their body hair and developed a layer of sub-cutaneous fat like other aquatic mammals to protect them from the cooler temperatures of the water. Today, we still have this layer of sub-cutaneous fat.

VACCINATION DANGERS

Most people are unaware of the dangers of childhood vaccinations. In 1998, strong evidence for a link between the MMR (mumps, measles, rubella) vaccination, autism and bowel disease in children was announced by UK doctors. In a further study, led by Professor John O'Leary, the measles virus was found in the intestines of 24 out of 25 children who developed 'autistic enterocolitis. This was after an apparently healthy infancy (31). *"The findings raise urgent new concerns over the safety of [the] MMR vaccine – the combined mumps, measles and rubella vaccination given routinely to hundreds of thousands of children every year"*. Some of the doctors who discovered the link were warned not to talk to the press about the findings and were shunned by 'experts' in the medical research council.

There is no scientific evidence that vaccines can be credited with eliminating any childhood disease. Epidemiological research, the study of disease and health in populations, shows that better nutrition, clean water, sanitation and better living conditions are responsible for the drop in disease. Dr. Robert Mendlesohn MD once said *"There has never been a single vaccine in this country [the USA] that has ever been submitted to a controlled scientific study. They never took a group of 100 people who were candidates for a vaccine, gave 50 of them a vaccine and left the other 50 alone to measure the outcome. And since that hasn't been done, that means if you want to be kind, you will call vaccines an unproven remedy. If you want to be accurate, you'll call people who give vaccines 'quacks'"*(32).

Not only are they probably non-effective, there is growing evidence that vaccines *cause* autism, allergies, epilepsy, learning disorders, ADD, ADHD, asthma, diabetes, dyslexia, hearing problems, vision problems, digestive disorders, stuttering and developmental delays. Many of the conditions associated with the psychic children. Vaccine damage creates inflammation at the base of the brain, which causes the 'insulation' or myelin sheath that protects the nerves to dissolve. The brain then short-circuits which affects many bodily functions. Researchers and doctors have noticed the similarities of autism and brain dysfunction to toxic poisoning. The toxic substances that linger in vaccines are due to a surprising production procedure. After the 'live' virus has been aquired, it must then be attenuated, or weakened for human use. The virus is passed through animal tissue several times to reduce its potency. The polio virus is passed through monkey kidneys; the measles virus is passed through chick embryos; and the rubella virus is passed through the dissected organs of an aborted human foetus! Foreign genetic material that is passed through animal cells can potentially alter our genetic makeup and mutate our DNA.

The weakened virus is then strengthened with antibody boosters and stabilisers. This process uses drugs, antibiotics and toxic disinfectants such as; neomycin, streptomycin, sodium chloride, sodium hydroxide, aluminium hydroxide, aluminium hydrochloride, sorbitol, hydrolysed gelatin, formaldehyde and thimerosal (mercury). Microscopic amounts of aluminium, formaldehyde and mercury can lead to cancer, neurological damage and death. But still our children are injected with them.

Unexpected animal viruses can jump the species barrier as well. This happened in the nineteen fifties and sixties when millions of people got infected with the SV-40 virus from monkeys. SV-40 is an immunorepressor and trigger for HIV. It is said to create the same symptoms as AIDS, and has been found in brain tumors, leukaemia and various cancers. It is considered a cancer-causing virus. According to Dr.Harris Coulter, nearly 20% of children are neurologically damaged by vaccination (33).

Vaccinations are 'pushed' on to children in schools and at the doctor's surgery. There is no scientific proof they actually do what they are supposed to do, so why bother taking them? According to the medical profession and the government, vaccines are essential for children to protect them from diseases, but when we look at the evidence, *not* having vaccinations is the more healthy option. ***I repeat, there is no scientific proof that vaccinations prevent the diseases they say they do***. There is also evidence that vaccines do not stay in the body for very long, as they are supposed to. So lets look at another side to the debate.

In the UK, vaccinating your child is often a requirement for staying on your GP's list. He is paid a bonus of £2,235 if 90% of the children under two years old get jabs. If only 70% are vaccinated, the bonus shrinks to £745; any smaller percentage means he gets a fraction of the amount (34). This is the same 'bribery' that is presented to doctors to get children on Ritalin. We really have to educate ourselves about what our growing children are ordered to take. We cannot blame our GPs, they are just the blind following the blind. Homeopathic remedies are believed to be the safest alternative.

Many parents have been charged with murdering their babies due to 'shaking them to death', but there is substantial evidence that vaccinations are the cause of Shaken Baby Syndrome (SBS). Some parents have even been convicted and imprisoned. But it has been discovered that the internal head injuries of SBS can only be sustained from:

a) being violently shaken (child abuse)
b) a combination of medical problems exacerbated by a serious vaccine adverse event;
c) a lone serious vaccine adverse event. (35).

So lets get some clarity on this. If your child has already had vaccinations, getting them on a nutrient-rich diet is essential. The following section covers the basics. Children who get measles are often deficient in vitamin A. Getting them on carrot juice or other orange vegetables can help. Vitamin A deficiency has also been linked to the contracting of polio. Breastfeeding your child for as long as possible is also helpful for those that are considering any vaccination, because it strengthens the child's immune system in the long run.

A good place to start would be a search on the Internet and the references at the back of this book.

NUTRITIONAL RECOMMENDATIONS

Organic food. Fresh non-organic produce has been found to have very high levels of pesticides. Although organic food is slightly more expensive, is it not worth paying a little extra for that peace of mind? Food co-ops are popping up all over the place. They only put a 10% mark-up on the wholesale price they bought it for. The more we buy organic, the more likely the prices will start dropping, even in supermarkets. And why not start growing your own food? It could be worth it in the long run. To find out where these co-ops are check out: sustainweb.org, cooperatives-uk.coop and colc.co.uk/Cambridge/ccda.

When organic produce is not available, foods that have less pesticides include: aubergines, peppers, frozen peas, cabbages, garlic, leeks, radishes, marrow, turnips and sweetcorn. Eating seasonal produce also reduces your exposure to anti-fungal and anti-bacterial chemicals mainly used to extend shelf-life. Wash ALL fruit and veg, even if it claims to be 'ready-washed' (36). Remove the outer leaves of lettuces also. Lettuces need more pesticides and chemicals because they lose their structural integrity quickly.

ESSENTIAL FATS

The British government has proposed to spend 300 million pounds on children and adolescents with mental health problems (37). How much of this will go into educating people about basic nutrition remains a mystery. If the government knew about essential fatty acids (EFAs), basic supplementation and the toxic overload we have already discussed, the money could be spent on things such as setting up healthy canteens at schools, or even employing nutritionists to teach children nutrition and healthy food preparation.

Essential fatty acids are vital in children's growth. They provide a plethora of nutrition and brain support that exceeds all other foods. Alpha-linolenic acid (omega 3) and linoleic acid (omega 6) are the two fats that form two of the 50 essential nutrients our body needs. The rarer and most important oil, omega 3, can mainly be found in oily fish (sardines, mackerel), flax seeds, hemp seed and other seeds and nuts. omega 6 is found in good quality vegetable oil, nuts and seeds. We usually get more omega 6 in our diet unless we love fish or flax seeds, but there is one seed (and oil) that holds the perfect balance for humans.

The hemp seed is a unique food. It contains all the essential amino acid proteins in a balanced ratio, that are vital to a vegetarian and vegan diet. The hemp seed shell contains high amounts of dietary fibre, which is vital for digestion. The main nutritional advantage is the balance of essential fats – omega 3, omega 6, omega 9 and GLA, which are useful in hundreds of conditions. Omega 3 is mainly found in oily fish, omega 6 in vegetable oils, omega 9 in olive oil and gamma linoleic acid (GLA) in evening primrose oil. But hemp has them all in a ratio that is designed for us humans. Hemp oil is *"natures most perfectly balanced oil"* according to author and nutritionist Udo Erasmus. It also contains vitamin E, minerals and life giving chlorophyll. Flaxseed (linseed) oil is richer in Omega 3, so a mixture of hemp and flax oil is recommended for children if vegetable oil is already used in the diet. Keep the oil in the fridge after opening. Do not cook with it because it destroys the EFAs. Use it on salads and dressings. One or two teaspoons per day is enough. newhuman.co.uk distributes an Omega 3 supplement for children that is sweetened with Xylitol and has a fruit flavour, called *Junior Max*.

In human brain development and function, scientists and nutritionists agree that essential fats play an important role in helping with conditions such as dyslexia, hyperactivity, ADD, dyspraxia (affects movement and memory), autism and other conditions. All of which are related to the phenomenon of the psychic children. EFAs have also been found to correct criminal behaviour and help show marked improvement in various mental illnesses. Symptoms of EFA deficiency include excessive thirst, dry skin, brittle hair and nails and blood sugar problems. Look out for these with your children.

NATURAL NUTRITION

In Chinese medicine theory, children with ADHD and related conditions are deficient in Yin. Yin represents the calm and receptive dimension of personality (37). A whole food diet plays a large role in building Yin essence. As we have seen, refined sugar and grains, pesticides, additives, preservatives, colourings and toxins all contribute to these conditions and deplete Yin, and thus need to be eradicated from the diet. Specific nutritional remedies that help, if given on a long term regular basis include sea vegetables (Nori, Arame, Hijiki, Kelp, Dulse, Kombo, Wakame), which supply a wealth of vital minerals essential in calming the body and mind, and can be cooked into stews and soups; also, many ADHD children have benefited from taking kelp tablets on a daily basis (ibid).

Foods such as spirulina, tempeh, almonds and butter help build the Yin essence. Omega 3 oils can also help. ADHD is also frequently made worse by parasitic infections. Colloidal silver and aloe vera gel can help with this; garlic is often used, but can eat up the precious yin essence due to its fiery nature. Children can often grow out of these conditions if proper dietary and emotional support is constantly available. The best book I've found that describes all these aspects is *Healing with Whole Foods* by Paul Pitchford. Colloidal silver is an incredible anti-bacterial and anti-viral substance, and well worth looking in to.

Micro-algae such as spirulina and chlorella are useful in childhood nutrition. Both are high in omega threes and GLA oils. GLA is important in general growth and development. Spirulina is recommended for those that were not breast-fed, in order to help hormonal and mental development that may have never occurred because of lack of vital nutrition during infancy (39).

VITAMINS AND MINERALS

Certain vitamin and mineral deficiencies are prevalent in children with ADHD and related conditions. These include the minerals zinc and magnesium that have been found to successfully treat ADD and hyperactivity. **Vitamins B6, B3 (niacin), folic acid** and **B1 (thiamine)** are also often deficient in children with these conditions. It has been found that manganese (not magnesium) causes irritability and difficulty concentrating. Various research has shown that supplementation of these nutrients decreases delinquent behaviour and leads to a significant improvement in academic abilities and behaviour (40).

Zinc is called the intelligence mineral because it is needed for optimal development and functioning of the brain and nervous system. It plays a role in protein synthesis and collagen formation; it is involved in the blood-sugar control mechanism and thus protects against diabetes; it is also needed for a healthy reproductive system. Zinc is a key component in numerous vital enzymes and plays a role in immune system maintenance. Phytates found in soy products, seeds and nuts interfere with zinc absorption more completely than with other minerals (if soaked or slightly roasted nuts and seeds lose the phytates) (41). The therapeutic range of zinc for children is 5-10mg. Zinc amino acid chelate, zinc citrate and picolinate are better than zinc sulphate or oxide (42). Foods rich in zinc include ginger root, pecan nuts, haddock, shrimps, turnips, brazil nuts, egg yolk, rye, oats, peanuts and almonds (ibid).

Magnesium strengthens bones and teeth, promotes healthy muscles to relax and is involved in harmonizing the nervous system and energy production (ibid P.311). In some studies of children age 7 to 12, those who took magnesium supplements showed a significant decrease in hyperactivity, compared to control groups who took a placebo (43). Carbonated drinks such as cola and other processed foods contain phosphoric acid, which leaches magnesium from the body. It is best if avoided, so check the labels. The therapeutic range for magnesium is 400-800mg. Good food sources include most nuts and seeds, cooked beans, sprouted grains and beans, garlic, raisins, green peas, wheat-germ, potato skins and crabmeat.

One study that Doreen Virtue mentions in her book found that 95% of ADHD children were deficient in magnesium (see note 5). It was also found that they were deficient in iron, copper and calcium. The researchers concluded "*It is necessary to supplement trace elements in children with hyperactivity*" (43). Therefore a good quality multi-mineral is recommended on a daily basis. The best one I have found on the market is called Maximol Solutions from Neways. It contains the most comprehensive array of easily absorbable ionic minerals with added natural vitamins, amino acids, phytochemicals and fruit juices. It also tastes good, so children can take it. newhuman.co.uk distributes it worldwide.

B vitamins are vital for proper brain function and development and have been used for children with ADD and ADHD. A great source of B-vitamins are sprouts such as mung beans, aduki, alfalfa and lentil sprouts. They also contain enzymes that aid digestion and amino acid proteins.

B3 (niacin) is essential for energy production, brain function and has been used successfully in controlling schizophrenia. It helps balance blood sugar levels and aids in digestion. Therapeutic range is 25-50mg for children. It is found in mushrooms, tuna, asparagus, cabbage, tomatoes, mackerel, courgettes, squash and cauliflower.

B6 stimulates serotonin release in the brain. Children who are hyperactive have lower serotonin levels than those who are not. Low serotonin can result in lethargy, depression and cravings for food (ibid P.154). B6 increases serotonin levels in children to a balanced level. It has been reported that tests were carried out that compared serotonin levels with children on Ritalin to those taking B6. The children on B6 maintained the levels even after they stopped taking it, whereas the Ritalin children did not show any raised levels at all. The therapeutic dose for children is 25-125mg. Foods include watercress, cauliflower, cabbage, peppers, bananas, squash, broccoli, asparagus, kidney beans, lentils, onions, seeds and nuts.

B12 is essential if the child is vegetarian. One fifty microgram tablet per week is sufficient. It can also be found in fortified margarine, soya milks, eggs and cheese.

These are basic recommendations for children. For a more detailed and personal supplement/diet program, please contact the author or a qualified nutritional advisor.

BENEFICIAL BACTERIA

Dr. Natasha Campbell-McBride's book *Gut and Psychology Syndrome – Natural treatment for Autism, Dyspraxia, ADD, Dyslexia, ADHD, Depression and Schizophrenia* is set to become a bestseller for parents who have children with any of these conditions. I saw her do a short talk at a nutrition conference where she was involved in the launch of a new advanced probiotic formula to the UK market. As a parent of a child diagnosed with learning disabilities, she has become acutely aware of the difficulties facing other parents like her, and she has been devoting her time to these families through The Cambridge Nutrition Clinic since 1998. She says *"The child's digestive system holds the key to the child's mental development"*.

According to McBride, The underlying issue, which can manifest itself in different children with different combinations, resides in the gut. So disorders such as autism, ADHD, dyspraxia, dyslexia, ADD, allergies and eczema are what Dr. Natasha Campbell-McBride calls 'Gut & Psychology Syndrome' or 'GAP Syndrome'. There is also another group under the same umbrella: Schizophrenia, depression, manic depression (bi-polar disorder) and obsessive-compulsive disorder. The book describes the way she has developed her treatments with the underlying focus on the gut-brain connection. By looking at all these disorders and noticing that virtually all her clients also had digestive abnormalities, she discovered the connection. Father of modern psychiatry, French psychiatrist Phillipe Pinel (1745 – 1828) wrote in 1807 that *"The primary seat of insanity is in the region of the stomach and intestines"*.

Digestion problems often start when weaning or when breast-feeding is stopped and infant formula has begun. These changes are mainly remembered in the second year, but parents often recall colic, vomiting (reflux) and other digestive symptoms from an earlier period. Early bloating and flatulence can cause severe pain in children, but is often not noticed or communicated; especially by autistic children who seem to develop self-punishing habits as a reaction to the discomfort.

By looking at how the immune system becomes compromised with vaccinations and to the ignorant dietary habits based upon sugar and refined flours, the book encapsulates a stunning and convincing theory of why many of these disorders are manifesting in modern society. By looking at the bigger picture it is clear that eating habits, farming methods and lifestyle changes over the last few decades are behind the cause of many mental disorders and learning difficulties. Allergens in wheat and dairy are contenders for the 'worst' food we can eat because of the way that they get through the gut wall and into the bloodstream, especially if the gut flora is not able to do its job. These allergens are often found in these children and are linked to poor brain and immune functioning and are a precursor to many of these issues.

Beneficial bacteria in the gut has many important roles. It maintains the health and integrity of the gut, protects from unwanted bacterial invaders, modulates the immune system and helps deal with toxins and heavy metals. If it is not in a good balance, the problems start to occur. Antibiotics, drugs, the contraceptive pill, sugar, refined foods, pollution, dental work, alcohol, disease and bottle-feeding are all responsible for damaging gut flora.

In the 1960's and 70's breast-feeding was unfashionable and many children have had to suffer the consequences. Breast-feeding establishes gut flora for life and enhances the immune system to a high degree. Babies are born with a sterile gut, so breast-feeding is the natural way for the gut to become populated with the best bacteria in the correct amounts. Bottle-fed babies guts are populated by unnatural bacteria in the wrong amounts that can lead to digestive issues later in life.

Beneficial bacteria in the gut produces essential nutrients such as vitamins B1, B2, B3, B5, B12, Biotin and Vitamin K. It also keeps the gut wall strong so allergens cannot get through and it helps nutrient absorption from foods and supplements. Many people who take supplements cannot absorb them because of gut flora abnormalities. The importance of probiotics in McBride's research is overwhelming. This is why she helped develop a supplement that was able to help with these conditions. "*Probiotic bacteria are essential in order to help people with all sorts of health problems: children with learning disabilities, adults with depression and other psychological conditions, people with digestive and immune system disorders, patients with ME, chronic fatigue syndrome, Fibromyalgia, MS and other neurological conditions. The list can go on. I see excellent results in my clinic every day."*

Dr.Natasha Campbell-McBride's website is medinform.co.uk and her book and specialist supplements are available from newhuman.co.uk.

ETHERIUM GOLD

As well as being a useful tool for ascension and DNA activation (see next chapter), Etherium Gold is now at the centre of research regarding learning and behaviour disorders in children. These graphics show electrical impulses of the brain before and after ingesting Etherium Gold. Notice the 'calmer' graphs on the right and the balancing of the red and blue. Etherium Gold has been found to work as soon as it bonds with the saliva in the mouth. So before you sit an exam or need to concentrate for extended periods, take a small amount of this incredible substance. Tests were carried out by The Alpha Learning Institute on a sophisticated 2-channel electro-encephalograph (EEG) that measures brain wave activity.

EEG BEFORE Etherium Gold

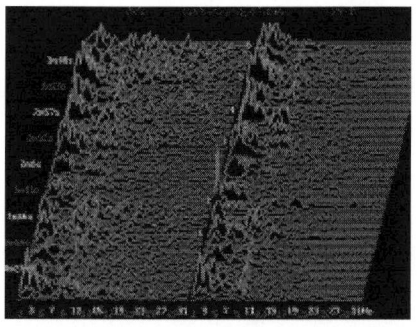 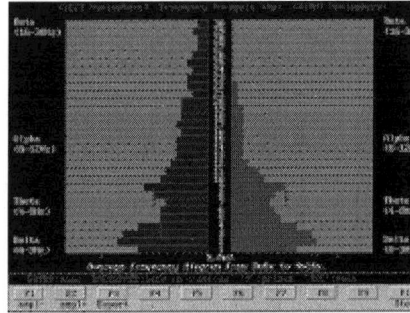

EEG AFTER 12 Etherium Gold Pills Over 3 Days

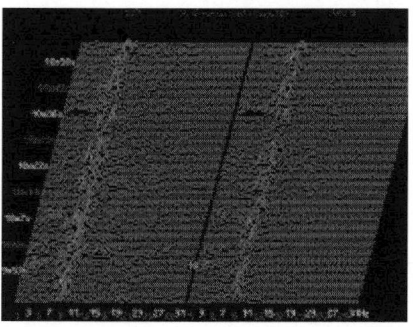 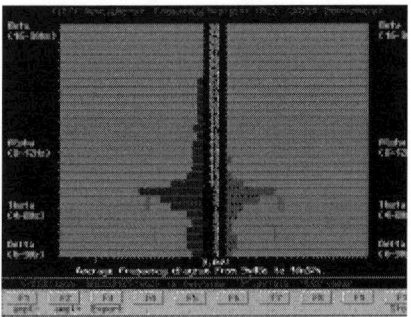

There is a distinct increase in left right balance and the increased emphasis on the alpha range between 7-10 hertz -- the learning wave. It is now accepted scientific fact that alpha brain waves are associated with greater intelligence, enhanced mind/body coordination, greater creativity, and less stress. The effects are virtually identical on all subjects, even when smaller amounts were tested. There are 2 main effects:

"Increased balance between the left and right hemisphere of the brain. This is the "holy grail" of all meditative and martial arts practices. Gravitation to alpha -- 7-12 Hz. Higher frequencies declined and lower frequencies increased. This is the "holy grail" of all specialists in reading, memory and learning. The ability to learn is maximized in the alpha range". (44)

The same results have been coming in from various test centres. The Mind Spa carried out preliminary research in 1998 and got identical results (45).

It is the connection to children with ADD, ADHD, ODD, autism and dyslexia that has got me interested. Research Director at the Alpha Learning Institute, Sean Adam confirms how effective Etherium Gold is for children with ADHD.

"Our research also clearly shows that left-right brain imbalances are predominating in many mental, behavioral dysfunctions such as dyslexia and attention deficit hyperactive disorders (ADHD). It is my professional opinion that Etherium Gold would be of tremendous benefit in any of these conditions and the most obvious answer as a healthy alternative to chemicals [such as Ritalin] *with harmful side effects."*

This discovery was confirmed by a mother of a hyperactive child in London:

"My ten year old son Alex has been suffering from ADHD since he was a tiny child. He was practically born running. Needless to say, his hyper-activity drove me insane and had a disruptive effect in his classroom. I was always being called in to discuss his behavior.

Despite his inability to sit down and focus, I was aware that he was a particularly bright child due to his articulate speech and astute observations, however, he was doing poorly in class and I was naturally very concerned. I took him to a multitude of doctors, child psychologists, neurological testers, behavioral therapists etc.

He was officially diagnosed with ADHD and was put on Ritalin, which I was very apprehensive about having read many controversial things about the drug as well as being personally opposed to children being dependent on drugs. The Ritalin did have an effect. He did calm down considerably. He also had trouble sleeping. But I saw no real marked difference in his performance at school. He was still way behind in spelling and was assigned a tutor to deal with his learning difficulties. This all had a very negative impact on his self-esteem. He struggled so, but simply wasn't improving.

When I became aware of the various positive effects of Etherium Gold I knew I wanted to try it on Alex as I had been determined to wean him off the Ritalin, as I was feeling more and more uncomfortable about administering it to him. The results were almost immediate. He has now been taking one capsule a day (morning) for almost a year now and the effect has been nothing short of miraculous. He is considerably calmer (not a drugged stupor like with the Ritalin) and most importantly, he is doing phenomenally well in school. His spelling, although still difficult, has improved drastically and he received the highest scores in his class on his SATs science exam. Previously he wasn't interested in reading at all, much to my disappointment, now I can't keep him in books. If before he couldn't sit still long enough to read or focus, he now reads for hours on end.

In addition, I present the gold to him as a vitamin, he doesn't suffer the stigma of being dependent on a drug for his intelligence, which is how he felt, despite my protesting the contrary. I also have been giving him fish oils as a supplement, which I have read helps quite a bit as many children's brains lack enough fatty acids to function as they should. The combination is fantastic and has changed our lives."

MOBILE PHONES & MASTS

Mobile phone technology is on the increase, and so is the number of children using them. The dangers of the radiation that is emitted from mobile phones has got researchers concerned about the potential damage they can cause to the developing brain and nervous system. Scientists have discovered that a call lasting two minutes can alter the natural electrical activity of a child's brain for up to an hour afterwards (46). A child's skull is still forming and is much more porous than an adults and doctor's fear that disturbed brain activity in children could lead to psychiatric and behavioural problems or impair learning ability (ibid).

The still-developing nervous system and associated brain-wave activity in a child (especially epileptics) are more vulnerable to dangers than adults. The repetition of the frequency of 8.34Hz and the pulsing of 2Hz, lie in the alpha and delta brain-wave signatures, respectively. By the age of 12, the delta waves disappear and the alpha rhythm becomes stabilized. So mobile phone use before age 12 confuses the bio-circuitry of the brain and can therefore lead to impaired brain-wave activity (47). The DNA and immune system become degraded by mobile phone use and from the radiation emitted from phone towers (ibid). Cancers, tumours and childhood leukaemia have all been linked to mobile phone use. A recent report by the Environmental Health Trust concluded that a few minutes exposure to mobile phone radiation can transform a 5% tumour into a 95% active cancer (48).

There are many devices that claim to reduce radiation from mobile phones, but is it really worth the risk to allow your children to use one?

Mobile phone masts are appearing all over the UK. Many schools now have masts within their grounds. The potential danger of these masts, when near humans, has got many parents concerned. All independent researchers in the field agree that the radiation coming from these masts are responsible for a rising tide of ill-health and have generally established that 500 metres is a safe distance to be from them. The US, New Zealand and Australian governments have already banned the erection of masts in residential areas.

A friend of mine in South East London campaigned against O_2 putting up a mast directly next to her son's school. She won the battle, but soon found out that the next school down the road had the same one erected there! So why are schools being targeted? The phenomenon of the Psychic children may hold the answer. The evidence throughout this chapter is suggesting there is pressure on companies to create ill-health, especially in children. Perhaps it is ignorance and mis-use of technology, but the facts suggest there may be ulterior motives behind it.

In September 2002, a group of EC doctors published a document about their own patient's illnesses and their link to mobile phone/mast radiation, called *The Freiberger Appeal.* They found *"...after carefully-directed inquiry, a clear temporal and spatial correlation between the appearance of disease and exposure to pulsed high-frequency microwave radiation..."* such as that from phone masts, intensive cell phone use and indoor cordless phones, are linked to *"a dramatic rise in severe and chronic disease among our patients".* These include: learning, concentration and behavioral disorders (including ADD and ADHD), extreme fluctuations in blood pressure, heart rhythm disorders, heart attack and strokes among an increasingly younger population, alzheimers, epilepsy, leukaemia, brain tumors and dramatic increases in less serious conditions. This is only a fraction of the available evidence. Other effects include: cataracts, retina damage, eye cancer, rapid cell ageing, cellular DNA repair interference, scalp nerve damage, joint pain, multiple sclerosis, digestive problems, asthma, thyroid conditions, embryo damage, miscarriages and even suicide (ibid).

Transmitters are popping up everywhere. They are even hidden in street signs, fake tree's, petrol stations and church spires. These following companies secretly erect them: Shell, Texaco, McDonalds, Trusthouse Forte, The Church of England, Branningtons, Wetherspoons and Network Rail. Boycotting them is a good start, but don't tell them I said so.

Orgone Generators are a simple to make device that have been recently (re)discovered that transforms 'deadly orgone radiation' (mobile phones, phone towers, TV's etc) into harmless chi (etheric energy, prana, life force). There are hundreds of devices in the new-age market scene that make similar radical claims. But this one really works and costs virtually nothing to construct. All you need is metal shavings, polyester resin, a double-terminated quartz crystal and a pyramid/cone/cup shaped mould.

To explain this properly, we have to go back to the research of Willhelm Reich, who in the 1950s was inventing 'Orgone Accumulators' and 'Cloud-Busters'. This was all orgone technology (orgone is chi, prana, life-force) that manipulated the energy force that is all around us and in us. But things have taken a step forward in the last few years thanks to a brave neo-anarchist called Don Croft. He has altered the designs of Reich and others and come up with several devices that reduce radiation, prevent mind control frequencies affecting us and even break up chem-trails that are being sprayed all over our countries. Croft is so notorious now, that if he were to be 'disappear in mysterious circumstances' he would become a martyr for the cause. To get a full download of his incredible journey with these devices check educate-yourself.org. It is spellbinding reading.

Small orgone generators called 'Tower Busters', no bigger than a plastic cup, are being placed near mobile phone masts to prevent the negative frequencies spreading into human life. They literally transform 'deadly orgone radiation' (DOR) into healthy orgone radiation (OR). The alchemical process outlines how they work. A combination of non-organic (metal) and organic materials are used (the resin is partly organic). The crystal balances the chaotic energy and enables the device to be programmed. When the resin begins to harden it produces excessive DOR, but when it is fully hardened, the frequency reverses and it starts producing healthy orgone radiation. Whenever DOR is in its vicinity, it 'sucks' it in and transmutes it to OR. An example of perfect alchemy.

These devices can be placed in your home as a general protector and are believed to stretch several hundred metres. Don Croft has got all the stories regarding modern orgone technology, but if you want to get hold of some, go to orgonegeneration.com. They also produce pendants that can be worn near the thymus gland and increase the body's orgone field.

Plasmonic Technology 'Lightowers' are another avenue worth considering. These work in a similar way to orgone generators, but do not draw in DOR. It is claimed they produce a huge light-field (chi-field) when they are placed aligned to north. Depending on the size of the lightower, the light field can go from 75 metres to 75 miles. The entire eco-system starts to change. The overly acidic rain is neutralized and the alkalinity of the water influences growth of vegetation on the ground. In Australia, they have apparently increased the yield of crops, accelerated germination of seeds, cleansed lakes and ponds, helped reduce biological stress caused by microwave radiation and increase negative ions in the air (the good ions).

Plasmodic Products, a company set up in Australia produce the stainless steel devices. The Lightower consists of powerful non-hertzian natural receivers, subjecting the photon (high-vibrational light) to *"specific proprietary alterations"*. When aligned to magnetic north (exactly), the devices act like an antenna and produce a modulated frequency field like a huge dome of light (or chi). Other devices they produce are designed to reduce electro-magnetic radiation in offices (computers, strip lights etc), cars and the human body. The pendants, if placed on the thymus gland (above the heart) increase the light field of the body. Lightowers even increase the width of earth energy currents and ley lines. I was introduced by the British distributor and we tested it out in many different ways – muscle testing, dowsing and on ley lines and got consistently positive results. More stories are coming through about this new technology, so check out the website for further updates.

So we now have a comprehensive outline of health for the new children. We can see that DNA is getting affected by non-foods, radiation, vaccinations and other toxins. Now we have the facts on protecting ourselves and finding nutritional balance, so now we can explore the deeper aspects of what is going on at our cellular level.

Please Note: The information in this chapter is intended solely for educational and informational purposes and not as medical advice. We cannot advise you on any illness, but we can guide people on how to maintain health. Please consult a 'qualified' medical or health professional if you have queries about your health

5. DNA ACTIVATION

"I can say to you, in all sincerity, that among "us", within our cities and families, possibly within your body, there is a new species of human that is being birthed! This new species demonstrates within themselves the potential living within each individual sharing our world today". (1)
Gregg Braden

DNA is also known as deoxyribonucleic acid, pronounced dee-ox-ee-rye-bo-noo-clay-ic acid. It is a large molecule, shaped like a double helix and found primarily in the chromosomes of the cell nucleus. The DNA contains the genetic information of the cell. It forms a double helix, which are two elongated molecular chains (like staircases) that wrap around each other.

Our genetic code consists of approximately 3 billion letters that make up the instructions for all human genes. While this code varies among individual humans by only about 1%, these variations are a key factor in understanding what makes us susceptible to disease and what determines our lifespan and how we age. The sections of DNA called genes instruct our cells to make proteins, which perform all of the body's essential tasks, like breathing, and determine physical features, such as hair colour. There are approximately 100,000 genes residing within each double helix of DNA. DNA tells our cells what they have been, what they will continue to be, and what they will become. The DNA is the blueprint for our life processes. Each cell of our bodies contains the complete genetic code for the whole body. Human DNA is generally divided into 46 chromosomes (23 pairs), each one containing characteristic genes that distinguish one chromosome from another. Derived from the Greek words "Chromo" for colour and "Soma" for body, they are intensely coloured bodies in our cells. One member of each pair comes from the mother through the egg and one member of each pair comes from the father through the sperm. Human DNA is about three billion "base" pairs long. If you stretched the human chromosome out end-to-end, it would be about six feet. All 46 chromosomes are folded into a space of a few thousandths of a millimetre (super coil).

Chandra hinted that it is our DNA that holds the answer to why so many of the children have such incredible abilities, so I researched scientific papers, well-known books by authors such as Gregg Braden, Jeremy Narby and Dan Winter and scanned the Internet for all the information I could find. In June 2004, an article in the New England Journal of Medicine documented a boy of five from Germany who had a major genetic mutation. He is able to hold seven pounds of weight with his arms extended and has muscles twice the size of other kids his age. The boy's DNA was found to block production of a protein called myostatin, that limits muscle growth. The news comes seven years after researchers at Johns Hopkins University in Baltimore created buff "mighty mice" by "turning off" the gene that directs cells to produce myostatin. The Psychic Children seem to be the chosen prototypes for humanity whether they like it or not. This information leads me to ask the question: are our children being born with advanced DNA or is the mutation taking place within the lifetime of the individual?

Gregg Braden was the first author to document proof of genetic changes within a person's lifetime. In his groundbreaking book *Walking Between the Worlds*, Braden describes an incident that was first reported in the April 1995 issue of the American journal, *Science News*. Researchers at the University of California, Los Angeles, School of Medicine reported unambiguous evidence of a boy who tested positive for HIV twice - at 19 days of age and one month later. Yet by every measure, this kindergartner was HIV free for at least 4 years. There have been many other reports of children being born with HIV, then testing 'clear' a few months or years later. Braden explains: *"The virus is not lying dormant within the body, opportunistically awaiting an external cue to become active; it is eradicated from the body!"* (ibid).

In August 2005, the University of Chicago discovered that many children born from the early 1980's had two newly identified genes – Microcephalin and ASPM. Both these genes are said to regulate brain growth. 70% of the children tested had one of the two genes, and 30% had both of them. Interestingly, IQ tests echo this discovery, because it has been found that IQ scores of 150 to 160 are now reached by roughly 30% of children. 130 is the beginning of the genius range. The average IQ is between 90 – 110. This research suggest that these genes were present at the very early stages of human evolution, but have been lying dormant until the early 1980's.

Other symptoms worth mentioning are related to the food we eat. Those who are mutating into this higher frequency find they can no longer tolerate low vibrational food. Processed food, hydrogenated fats, e-numbers and refined grains are not welcome by a body that requires high vibrational nutrition. Our bodies are becoming magnetically lighter, so to honour this process we must examine what we are putting inside our bodies. We must also become aware of what is getting in to us through the surface of our bodies. Our skin acts like a sponge, so if we let the thousands of toxins and chemicals that are rife in household and cosmetic products into our genetic make-up, our DNA will be compromised.

DNA - THE FORGOTTEN CODES

During the 1950's, James D. Watson discovered the hidden matrix of our genetic make-up. He described the building blocks of life as specific combinations of oxygen, hydrogen, carbon and nitrogen. The 64 possible combinations mapped out in to what he called the *genetic code,* the basics of DNA. It was quickly noticed that there was a mystery within the code. Only 20 of the 64 combinations are 'enabled'. The others appear to be dormant, repeating sequences that get the same results (amino acid) every time.

The combinations that do work each produce a unique amino acid, which Gregg Braden describes as an *'antenna'*. Braden believes these antenna allow us to tune in and receive a unique quality of vibration. With only 20 of the 64 turned on, this suggests that the codons (combinations) have somewhere in the past lost their ability express uniquely. How this might have happened remains a mystery, but many exotic theories have been put on the table, such as ETs and genetic alterations in our distant past.

So what we have here are certain genetic codes that all lead to the same result or amino acid. What would human life be like if more of the codes were enabled? Would it go some way to explain the phenomenon of the psychic children and all their abilities? And how do we get those codons turned on? Several experiments that begin to answer these questions have been carried out by Dan Winter and the Heart Math Institute. One experiment worth noting involved twenty-eight people, who were all trained in techniques of generating a variety of strong emotions. They were all given a vial of DNA to focus these emotions on. What was discovered was that the DNA changed its shape according to the feelings generated by the researchers. When the researchers felt gratitude, love, and appreciation, the DNA responded by relaxing, and the strands unwound. The length of the DNA became longer. When the researchers felt anger, fear, frustration, or stress, the DNA responded by tightening up. It became shorter and switched off many of the DNA codes. The shutdown of the DNA and the codes was reversed and the codes were switched back on when the feelings of love, joy, gratitude, and appreciation were promoted and felt by the researchers (3).

Varying emotional states appear to affect the wave-length of the double helix. If you are in a state of love, the codons mirror the same wavelength as the DNA and they, in a manner of speaking, connect. Fear, on the other hand, has the opposite effect. The codons and the DNA go out of sync. They appear to be separated, only touching at certain intervals. So what does this mean?

If the codons are synchronised with the double helix, it allows more opportunities for certain amino acids to be formed at a healthy level. If they are out of sync, some of the amino acids will not be formed, which means the antenna are not picking up the vibrations the body may need. This vibration missing could be the one that stimulates the immune system, and if this is the case then HIV could flourish, without the immune system properly 'turned on'. Drunvalo suggests four more codons are activated with those that are immune to HIV and perhaps this is the case (4). Perhaps though, it could be to do with a realisation of their own mortality. This could help them open up to more love and compassion, because they know their time is short, which could 'relax' the DNA to enable it to become activated. Gregg Braden's research in to the ancient Essene texts has also suggested this scenario:

*"In the ancient traditions, there is a quality of emotion and feeling and thought that appears to optimize those genetic codes and "turn them on" thus giving us longevity, vitality and **tremendously-enhanced immune systems**. That quality is what we today call compassion. That is the common thread of emphasis through these ancient traditions, this science of compassion."* (5)

DNA is affected by the nature of our emotional state. Compassion, loving feelings, empathy, openness, truth, forgiveness and anything we call positive. These emotions affect our molecular structure. It becomes clear why the ancient texts (and the psychic children) recommend focussing on these positive emotions. Not only do they help us to stay physically healthy, they also propel us on the path to enlightenment. The DNA, when 'in tune', resonates to a higher vibration. This vibration is elevated to our consciousness. Our consciousness therefore becomes 'higher'. To put it simply, through being compassionate, we reach a higher state of consciousness. The Buddhists have known this all along.

I received an email shortly before I set about writing this chapter. It contained this beautiful nugget of wisdom; called, *A Story of Two Wolves*.

A Native American grandfather was talking to his grandson about how he felt about a tragedy. He said, "I feel as if I have two wolves fighting in my heart. One wolf is vengeful, angry and violent. The other wolf is loving and compassionate." The grandson asked him, "Which wolf will win the fight in your heart?" The grandfather answered, "The one I feed."

BLOOD TYPES & DNA

Drunvalo Melchizedek believes that alterations in diet and climate change led to a slightly different genetic make-up in various parts of the world. This then led to alteration in blood type and therefore our DNA. About 15,000 years ago we all had the blood type O flowing through our veins. We all killed animals for food. After the Atlantis catastrophe about 12,000 years ago, most of humanity stopped moving around and stayed in their local vicinity. We became farmers, so our diets also changed. We began eating food that we had never eaten before. The body mutated the DNA with these changes claims Drunvalo. Enzymes and stomach acids altered as we assimilated the new diet. This led to blood type A (6).

As changes in lifestyle and farming continued, blood types also mutated further until today where we have four major blood types – A, AB, B and O. Now we are in the 21st century, the foods we are eating are so varied that in one day we could eat food from ten different countries. Western society has opened the floodgates to dietary choice. What this suggests is that we are developing another blood type; a planetary blood type that stretches across all cultures. It has already been documented that DNA is mutating in humans all over the planet. Russia, China, America and Europe are all witnessing the DNA shift in the children, so what proof is there on a physical level that genetic mutation is really happening in relationship to the food we eat?

The liver deals with all the poisons and toxins that enter our body and regulates the production of the blood. According to Drunvalo, it is the liver that holds the key to this question. The liver is stronger than ever in these children. They can assimilate and process large quantities of junk food that contain e-numbers, toxins, hydrogenated fats etc. Basically, foods that do not function well with our current genetic make up. The response to this junk food diet is that the liver can now deal with this toxic overload. The liver has mutated to allow children to deal with their diet. Cockroaches, who at first react to poison, then mutate to deal with it, then even allow the poison to become its food are examples of how our children are dealing with their diet. Our children have to adapt to survive (ibid).

ANCIENT GENETICS

According to the research of authors such as Zechariah Sitchin and Alan Alford, we were once visited by the Nefilim, a group of beings from planet Nibiru some 450,000 years ago. They came here to mine our wealth of mineral deposits with a focus on gold. The reason for this has remained a mystery, but with the modern rediscovery of white powder gold and the other monatomic elements it is becoming clear they were not just plundering for material wealth (see next section).

It is also said that our DNA was altered to a degree that we would become workers for the Nefilim. There was so much gold to mine that they genetically engineered the humans to a cross-bred race of 'slaves' (who became our ancestors) to mine the mineral deposits. Genetic evidence for this is scarce, but a research team in California run by Dr Vilayanur Ramachandran in 1996 put a spotlight on this theory (7). It was suggested that there is a 'God Module' in our temporal lobes. His team believe that God (or gods) is a vital evolutionary component of the brains bio-circuitry – a Darwinian adaptation to impose stability and order on society to encourage co-operation between individuals.

Another take on this is the idea that we were programmed to be subservient workers following orders. This perhaps worked well whilst we had 'gods' around to do the ordering. But since the Nefilim left the planet, it has caused us such confusion, that we have rapidly descended into blood thirsty, irrational and aggressive beings with no direction. The history books provide the evidence for this part, but as we will see in the next section, the very thing we were programmed to mine could be the key factor in reversing this ancient genetic bondage.

WHITE POWDER GOLD

Sir Williams Flinders Petrie unearthed a temple on the Sinai Peninsula, at Mt Serabit, near Serabit El Khadim in 1903 that was full of alchemical iconography from the time of the 3rd Egyptian Dynasty. In this temple complex tons of white powder composed of monatomic platinum group elements was discovered. An alchemical crucible was also unearthed. In his most recent books (8), Laurence Gardner has focussed on these 'higher' metals and their use throughout history. In ancient Mesopotamia it was called *shem-an-na*. In Egypt it was called *Mfkzt* – which both roughly translate as *Highward Fire-stone,* while the Alexandrians venerated it as the *Paradise Stone*. The 'bread' or 'manna' described in numerous ancient texts refers to the monatomic metals that were used in initiations and ceremony.

Made into conical cakes, or suspended in water, as far back as 2180 BC, pharaohs were ingesting the gold to enhance their pineal activity and thereby to heighten their awareness, perception and intuition. It was also used to feed the light body (the Ka). The master metallurgists, who were adepts of various mystery schools were the alchemists in charge. The tradition of 'bread and wine' has travelled across the centuries. It is now becoming startlingly clear that this bread is monatomic gold. You may be aware of current churchgoers having a symbolic representation of bread placed under their tongue. This is an echo of the ancient use of gold in modern religious practice. It is also the correct way to ingest the substance. By allowing it to dissolve under the tongue, it enters the blood system without any disruption from the acids in the stomach and digestive system.

Conical presentation at the Sinai temple of Hathor (whitepowdergold.com)

The 15th century French alchemist Nicolas Flamel and the 17th century philosopher, Eirenaeus Philalethes (revered by Isaac Newton, Robert Boyle, Elias Ashmole and other Royal Society colleagues of his era), were both fully aware of the nature of white powder gold. They both realised they had discovered the Philosophers Stone. In his work from 1667 called *Secrets Revealed,* Philalethes wrote:

"Our Stone is nothing but gold digested to the highest degree of purity and subtle fixation. It is called a stone by virtue of its fixed nature; it resists the action of fire as successfully as any stone. In species it is gold, more pure than the purest; it is fixed and incombustible like a stone, but its appearance is that of a very fine powder" (9).

ORME'S AND M-STATE ELEMENTS

The Monatomic elements were rediscovered by wealthy cotton farmer David Hudson during his pioneering work into modern farming methods. Through a series of tests he realised he had discovered something quite remarkable. These elements were classified in the 1980's as ORME's (Orbitally Rearranged Monatomic Elements). New understandings in physics suggests the powders might actually be 'diatomic' or 'small atomic cluster condensates' They are generally referred to as ORME's or 'M-State Elements'(10). When heated the metals drop to 56% their original weight. 44% goes missing completely. It has been found that it actually goes into a different dimension. According to Gardner, the Egyptians called it the *Field of Mfkzt'* and the Mesopotamians called it the *Plane of shar-on'* – the super-conductive dimension of the *"Orbit of light"*(11). The M-State elements then start to levitate and create an anti-gravitational field in the near vicinity.

In the *Scientific American* journal of May 1995, the platinum metal ruthenium was discussed in relationship to human DNA. When single ruthenium atoms were placed at each end of the double-helix, it became 10,000 times more conductive to light (12).

White powder gold is a substance that resonates in this dimension as well as other 'higher' dimensions. Therefore if we ingest this, it connects us to our higher dimensional self. We are then able to access higher states of awareness, or vibrate at a higher frequency. Through the hormonal increase, our light body starts to be nourished, our cells become healthier, our DNA carries more light and we are able to access our higher self and become an observer of our mind – much like in meditation. As more light travels through ones body, our light body becomes activated and it creates an arena where growth through struggle becomes less and less. The light keeps shining whatever is happening in your life. The relaxed DNA enables this process of consciousness shifting to take place. We are able to become the observer or watcher of our reality. The psychic children seem to already be there on many levels. It is as though their DNA is already in this relaxed state or is in the process of relaxing and therefore activating the forgotten codes. As the rediscoverer of monatomic gold David Hudson quoted *"Alchemy deals with transformation down to the cells, to the DNA"* (9).

To get the full picture of the power of white powder gold, I started taking it as soon as I had finished a ten-day meditation course. The course is called *Vipassana* and is considered to be the closest example to the technique the Buddha taught (13). It enables one to become the observer of the mind and to detach from the many drama's our mind likes to play out. Through observation of bodily sensation and not reacting to them, one becomes peaceful and totally in the present moment.

White powder gold has similar qualities. Like in meditation, the gold brings one closer to the Alpha state of the brain, where the right and left-brain balance is harmonised. It is scientifically accepted that alpha brain waves are associated with greater intelligence, enhanced creativity, improved mind/body coordination and agility, and less stress. (14). This is why the Kings and Pharaoh's of the ancient world partook in the gold. It enabled them to deify themselves.

The gold had a strong effect on me. I was taking more than the recommended dose and found that my pineal activity was getting more noticeable by the day. Combined with the meditation, I was becoming very *tuned in*. My psychic ability and telepathy were becoming rampant to a point where I had a psychic overload. When I returned to the recommended dose, everything became calm and soon returned back to a level of balance. I was taking pure white powder gold from whitepowdergold.com. Recently I have been turned on to Etherium Gold and their related products that are naturally formed monatomic elements from an ancient seabed. These provide a balanced variation of the monatomic elements from a natural source.

Each monatomic element carries a certain vibrational frequency. Both iridium and rhodium have anti-ageing properties, while platinum elements and ruthenium interact with our cellular body and possibly activate 'junk DNA'. It is also now known that gold and the platinum metals activate the entire endocrine system, which gives heightened awareness, intuition and aptitude (15). As already mentioned, the pineal gland is stimulated which increases melatonin production. Melatonin enhances and boosts the body's immune system and is a cancer preventative. High melatonin production increases energy, stamina and regulates sleep patterns. It is a powerful antioxidant, and it has positive mental and physical anti-ageing properties (16).

The Etherium products make similar claims. Etherium Gold Powder contains monatomic elements of Gold (94 ppm), Iridium (24 ppm), Chromium (225 ppm), Silver (178 ppm), Rhodium (15 ppm) and Platinum (78 ppm). Although they are not produced the same way as the high spin monatomic elements, independent scientists have shown they still interact with our DNA and endocrine systems and produce the similar results. The Etherium gold has been tested by the Alpha Learning Institute in Switzerland and was found to have many of the properties of the alchemically produced gold. As well as helping one reach the Alpha state of the brain, it also helps us receive high vibrational information or channelling. It then allows our newly balanced left and right brain to assimilate this information at a cellular level.

Research into the health giving benefits of the monatomic compounds has startling connotations for the nature of modern medical practice. Cancer, ADD, ADHD and many other conditions are being treated with monatomic elements. So through the research into the nature of DNA, I now come back to the psychic children. ADD & ADHD can be treated with this incredible substance.

The Etherium Gold is the medicine that many children with these conditions can be helped with, but do the scientific establishment really want all the potential revenue for drugs such as Ritalin be handed over to the producers of the gold? And do the powers-that-be want to see our children evolve even quicker on the path to the light than they already are? This is a double-edged sword that has presented itself at the exact right time for the health and evolution of our species.

If Zechariah Sitchin is correct, perhaps the gold is part of our ascension process, re-establishing our genetics to their original state. With only a small percentage of our DNA activated, the gold could help activate our genetic potential. Not only can our children overcome ADD and ADHD, but our DNA has the opportunity to become what it originally was – *divine*. Research is already being carried out into our future genetic potential. The so-called *junk DNA* is under the spotlight by a group of Russian scientists, linguists and geneticists in a venture to explore this un-chartered genetic territory.

RUSSIAN 'JUNK DNA' RESEARCH

Russian biophysicist and molecular biologist Pjotr Garjajev and his colleagues have been carrying out cutting-edge research into the more esoteric nature of DNA. A majority of genetic scientists believe that about 90% of our DNA does not does function in any way and follows the same codes. The 10% they can document and thoroughly test is visible to them in experiments. Therefore, what cannot be 'scientifically' documented is left on the shelf, suggesting they simply do not understand what it is for. But the scientists in Russia have been exploring 'mysteries' and psychic abilities for decades. Garjajev's group, who have been studying DNA, focussing on the 90% that is classed as 'junk' DNA simply did not believe that our DNA is useless. The latest research *(into junk DNA)* explains phenomena such as clairvoyance, intuition, spontaneous and remote acts of healing, self healing, affirmation techniques, unusual light-auras around people (namely spiritual masters), mind's influence on weather-patterns and much more (2).

Immediately we can see many classic traits of the Psychic children. The research in Russia is helping people realise the true nature of our genetic structure, rather than be told we are 90% redundant by western scientists. If extra DNA is activated, it certainly looks like it does more than enhance the immune system. The 'antennae' are picking up on vibrations far beyond the sensitivity of electronic instruments. Are the codons that are not activated part of our future, and not part of our past as agreed upon by most scientists? Are we stepping into realms that our species has never entered before? It is beginning to look like this may be the case.

When placed in a vacuum, the Russian scientists found that DNA caused disturbances in space/time that then produced magnetized wormholes! These are the microscopic versions of what is left by burned-out stars, commonly termed Einstein-Rosen bridges in the vicinity of black holes. These are thought to be tunnel connections between different parts of the Universe that allow information to travel in and out of space and time. The DNA somehow attracts these pieces of information and passes them on to our consciousness. This phenomenon is called 'Hyper-communication', where information is passed inter-dimensionally. It is as though the DNA acts as a 'stargate' between this dimension and others. In the book *Vernetze Intelligenz*, there are several stories of how this information is downloaded via DNA. It also helps explain the phenomenon of *channelling*.

The Italian composer Giuseppe Tartini for instance dreamt one night that a devil sat at his bedside playing the violin. The next morning Tartini was able to note down the piece exactly from memory, he called it the Devil's Trill Sonata. For years, a 42-year old male nurse dreamt of a situation in which he was hooked up to a kind of knowledge CD-ROM. Verifiable knowledge from all imaginable fields was then transmitted to him that he was able to recall in the morning. There was such a flood of information that it seemed a whole encyclopaedia was transmitted at night. The majority of facts were outside his personal knowledge base and reached technical details about which he knew absolutely nothing (2).

It was also noted how this information can be passed between individuals whose DNA is 'turned on'. Telepathy is becoming a reality. This helps explain how many of the Psychic children can exchange complex concepts with each other through an invisible web. It is the DNA communicating over vast distances:

"We now know that just as on the Internet our DNA can feed its proper data into the network, can call up data from the network and can establish contact with other participants in the network. Remote healing, telepathy or remote sensing about the state of relatives etc. can thus be explained. Some animals know also from afar when their owners plan to return home. That can be freshly interpreted and explained via the concepts of group consciousness and hyper communication" (ibid).

The process of hyper-communication works best when one is in a relaxed state. As we have seen already, relaxation is the key to DNA function. Stress, worries and a fast mind prevent successful hyper communication. Meditation may be the best way to tune in with our DNA. In nature hyper-communication has been successfully applied for millions of years. The organized flow of life in insect states proves this dramatically. Modern man knows it only on a much more subtle level, as "intuition". But we, too, can regain full use of it. An example from nature: When a queen ant is separated from her colony, building still continues fervently and according to plan. If the queen is killed, however, all work in the colony stops. No ant knows what to do. Apparently the queen sends the 'building plans' also from far away via the group consciousness of her subjects. She can be as far away as she wants, as long as she is alive. In man hyper communication is most often encountered when one suddenly gains access to information that is outside one's knowledge base. Such hyper-communication is then experienced as inspiration or intuition.

When hyper-communication occurs, one can observe in the DNA as well as in the human being some interesting anomolies. Dr. Vladimir Poponin irradiated DNA samples with laser light. On screen a typical wave pattern was formed. When they removed the DNA sample, the wave pattern did not disappear, it remained. Many control experiments showed that the pattern still came from the removed sample, whose energy field apparently remained by itself. This effect is now called phantom DNA effect. It is surmised that energy from outside of space and time still flows through the activated wormholes after the DNA was removed (17).

A side-effect encountered in hyper-communication is inexplicable electromagnetic fields in the vicinity of the persons concerned. Electronic devices like CD players can be affected and cease to function for hours. When the electromagnetic field slowly dissipates, the devices function normally again. Many of the Psychic children have this effect on such devices.

THE COSMIC SERPENT

DNA communication is a subject that anthropologist, Jeremy Narby experienced whilst spending time with the Amazonian natives of Peru (18). Rather than just objectively study the tribes, he got involved in their shamanic culture and was soon regularly partaking in Ayahuasca ceremonies. Ayahuasca is a combination of psychoactive plants that are said to connect our consciousness with the DNA. However, it is a powerful "medicine" that is not suitable for everyone.

His initial research into the 'two serpents' that started appearing in his visions, opened up an unknown window into DNA research. Many people had similar experiences to Narby – seeing two snakes and communicating with them. He soon realised that his DNA was revealing itself through the ingestion of psychedelic plants. He noticed the resemblance of the double helix of DNA and the intertwined snakes. He found that many ancient cultures used a similar symbol that connected DNA to the 'snake' visions. This convinced him that the DNA is communicating with our consciousness and has been for a very long time.

Another part of his research focussed in on DNA communication between different species. The shamans had told him that it was the Ayahuasca that connected them to their DNA and this enabled interspecies communication between the various plants, animals and humans. Plant DNA was communicating with human DNA. The shamans would use this tool and ask their DNA to connect with the plant kingdom and find the relevant medicine for their client. The results were very specific and displayed an age-old tradition of inter-species communication. The odds of guessing the correct plant from the thousands available pushed this beyond the realms of chance. In the book *The Cosmic Serpent,* Narby concludes that modern DNA research needs another look. A whole different approach is needed to reveal the ultimate truth about our genes. The Amazonian shamans directly receive their knowledge from the ingestion of Ayahuasca. They believe that the plant itself is giving them the information. What can now be seen is that it brings the Shamans into a state of relaxation and awareness where their DNA begins communicating, just like in hyper-communication.

    I had the opportunity to partake in an Ayahuasca ceremony in my hometown of Glastonbury during the writing of this chapter. I had already tried some natural Dimethyltryptamine (DMT) some months ago and I experienced "death" three times! Inter-dimensional travel becomes very real on DMT, but it was the Ayahuasca that gave me the insights into DNA that I had heard so much about. Ayahuasca contains DMT and has a similar effect. The visions and hallucinations are simply outrageous. I was fortunate enough to take it with several good friends and seekers in a ceremony led by an Australian shaman called Darpan.

    The first time one takes the plant, a great deal of purging takes place. Physical and emotional trauma is released through vomiting and convulsions. When the plant is ready, it will introduce itself to you. But not before it has explored absolutely every part of your being. This was my experience anyway. It can be overwhelming and quite shocking, especially if you have not experienced psychedelics before. Ayahuasca is said to be the 'Mother' plant and can provide answers to any question one asks her.

    I asked about the nature of DNA, specifically my DNA, but to retrieve answers in such a profoundly strong experience was not easy. I saw snakes. I saw DNA. I saw mitochondria wobbling around in my field of vision. I even saw myself sitting at this desk writing this book. Sacred geometry came through in my visions on several occasions that correlated with what David Wilcock once told my friend Jake in a television conversation with him. He told him that the dodecahedron was the current building block of DNA. The reason the double helix spirals as it does in its specific configuration is due to the sides of the dodecahedron forming a chain at certain geometric frequencies. Remember what Chandra said at the conference? *"The dodecahedron in sacred geometry will help with understanding the alignments".*

Sacred geometry holds the key to understanding the nature of genetics. The way the cell divides and reproduces is all controlled by geometric principles. Our entire existence is governed by sacred geometry. Drunvalo gives an intelligent summary of the progression of life through sacred geometry and the platonic solids (19). It begins with the ovum, a sphere. We then move on to a tetrahedron with four cells, then on to a star tetrahedron at eight cells. From two cubes at sixteen cells we return to a sphere beginning at 32 cells, then from that we become as torus at 512 cells. The Icosahedron and dodecahedron do not play a part in the basics of cell division, but as we have seen, they both play an important role regarding the sacred geometries of the earth.

So we now have some ideas about what is happening to human DNA within our own bodies, but what are the external factors that are causing genetic mutation and ultimately DNA activation? Food and certain toxins are causing mutations within the lifetime of a human, but there is a macrocosmic game playing out in the heavens that the Maya knew about thousands of years ago.

6. GALACTIC ALIGNMENT 2012

DNA & SOLAR RADIATION

Biologist Charles Darwin was one of the first to describe the evolutionary process as one of natural selection, whereby the most capable flourish at the expense of the weak. Later, it was found that genetic changes, exaggerated by selective breeding, were the facilitating prime mover in the selection process. But Maurice Cotterell, author of *The Mayan Prophecies,* has studied the effects of solar radiation on humans for over twenty years and discovered that genetic mutations are caused through the action of ionising radiations. He has found that X-rays and gamma rays from the sun are the key factor in genetic leaps of species. The DNA is spliced which causes the genetic mutations. Ionising radiation and magnetic radiation from solar flares on the sun's surface have acted upon developing species causing mutational leaps.

In 1986 Cotterell put forward a revolutionary theory concerning astrology and sun cycles. For several years he suspected that the sun's variable magnetic field had consequences for life on earth. The sun has a complex field that loops and twists itself into knots. It has long been suspected that these loops give rise to sunspots, which are dark blemishes on the sun's skin. The number, size and location of sunspots are constantly changing and as a former radio officer, Cotterell was well aware that they have profound effects upon the earth's magnetic envelope, the magnetosphere.

Whilst working as Head of Electrical and Communications Engineering at Cranfield Institute of Technology, he devised a program that would compute the relationship between the sun's magnetic field and the earth. As expected his model predicted that there should be a sunspot cycle of roughly eleven and a half years, closely corresponding to what has been observed over several centuries. The most recent peak was supposed to happen in March to April 2000, with the following one expected in 2011. However it did not peak until February 2001, putting the next one back to 2012. Cotterell theorized that the peak of many greater cycles will coincide in December 2012 with a full solar magnetic reversal. This would trigger a magnetic field reversal and destroy the world, but there is no evidence to support this claim.

His earlier work on what he called *Astrogenetics* indicated that human fertility was dependent on the presence of sunspots. The sun not only affects our weather patterns and the earth's magnetic and polar stability, it also affects the *progress that we make as societies.* With these higher points of progress must also come greater creativity, intuition and insight, those very human traits necessary to bring about massive social change. These social changes could be lumped into the elusive category of "spiritual growth." There would obviously be a correlation with major advances in society and major personal advances in individuals (1). As we have already seen, DNA mutation can cause advances in individuals on a spiritual and physical level. The sunspot cycles are a natural part of this process of activating our DNA.

It does not end there with solar activity. Although these sun cycles are well established in certain scientific circles, the *extreme* activity in the sun preceeding the most recent sunspot peak of 2000 has got physicists alarmed. A team at the Rutherford Appleton Laboratory near Oxford, led by Dr. Mike Lockwood, has discovered that in the last century, the overall strength of the sun's magnetic field has more than doubled, becoming *230 percent stronger than it was in 1901* (2). Even more interestingly, this rate of magnetic field growth is continually increasing in speed.

The images below show the sun at solar minimum in 1996 and solar maximum in 1999. Although it was at its maximum between 1999 and February 2001, it was expected to decline in strength following 2001. But in the summer of 2002 it reached solar maximum again.

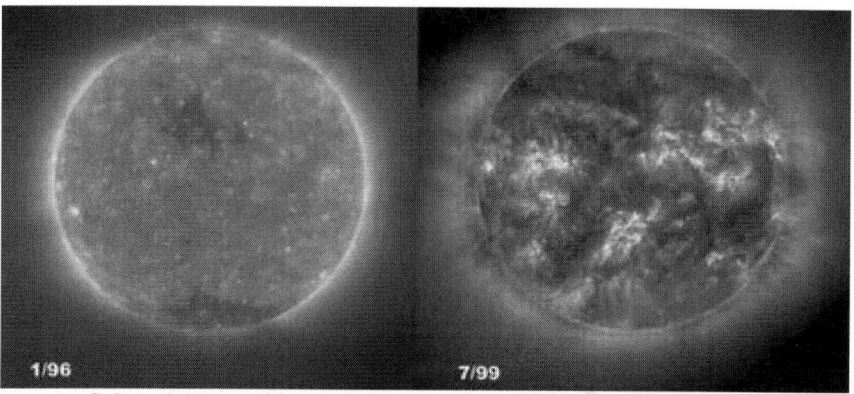

Solar minimum 1996 and solar maximum 1999 (Courtesy of NASA)

During the solar maximum of 1989, an X-ray flare of high-energy protons was emitted from the sun on March 5th facing directly to earth. This continued until March 13th. Not only did the earth's magnetic poles deviate by eight degrees (the most since 1952), it also caused major disruption of communication systems, created non-polar aurora borealis effects and even shut down the entire Canadian power grid (3). If we remember that the sun contains 99.86% of the mass in the solar system, then we can easily see that it wields the strongest thermal, gravitational and electromagnetic influence. Solar maximums have also been found to be linked to severe weather conditions, tornadoes, earthquakes and volcanic activity on earth. This observation is confirmed by scientists, Dr. Aleskey Dmitriev, Richard Pasichnyk (4) and Dr.N.A. Kozyrev (5).

Arguably, the ultimate energy release from our sun comes from what are known as *coronal mass ejections*. In these cases, the entire sun releases a super-flash of energy over much of its surface simultaneously, which travels out into space as a halo-like expanding bubble that can contain up to ten billion tons of electrified gas. Dr. Dmitriev explains that with each passing year, these super-flashes are actually traveling *faster* through space than ever before, suggesting *interplanetary space has become a better conductor.* The 'solar wind' carries these particles throughout the solar system, which affect the electromagnetic fields of all the planets. The planets then absorb this energy, which influences weather, earthquakes, internal heating, volcanic activity and even the brightness of planets. So what else has been happening to the planets in our solar system?

Sun: *More activity since 1940 than in previous 1150 years, combined*
Mercury: *Unexpected polar ice discovered, along with a surprisingly strong intrinsic magnetic field ... for a supposedly "dead" planet*
Venus: *2500% increase in auroral brightness, and substantive global atmospheric changes in less than 30 years*
Earth: *Substantial and obvious world-wide weather and geophysical changes*
Mars: *"Global Warming," huge storms, disappearance of polar icecaps*
Jupiter: *Over 200% increase in brightness of surrounding plasma clouds*
Saturn: *Major decrease in equatorial jet stream velocities in only ~20 years, accompanied by surprising surge of X-rays from equator*
Uranus: *"Really big, big changes" in brightness, increased global cloud activity*
Neptune: *40% increase in atmospheric brightness*
Pluto: *300% increase in atmospheric pressure, even as Pluto recedes* farther *from the Sun* (5)

None of these statistics are from "fringe" scientists. This report's scientific data, from a variety of highly credible institutions (including NASA), reveals that startling "climate change" effects are occurring, not just here on earth, but, in fact throughout the entire solar system. Wilcock points out that this material has been publicly available for nearly a decade in some cases, but it was simply never assembled into a coherent picture of *"a system in significant transition"* until he and Richard Hoagland assembled their version of events into a comprehensive hyper-dimensional view of our cosmos. See enterprisemission.com.

THE HELIOSPHERE

The heliosphere is formed by the magnetic field of the Sun. It creates a protective egg around our solar system as it hurtles through space. It is shaped like a massive teardrop, with the tail being dragged through space like that of a comet.

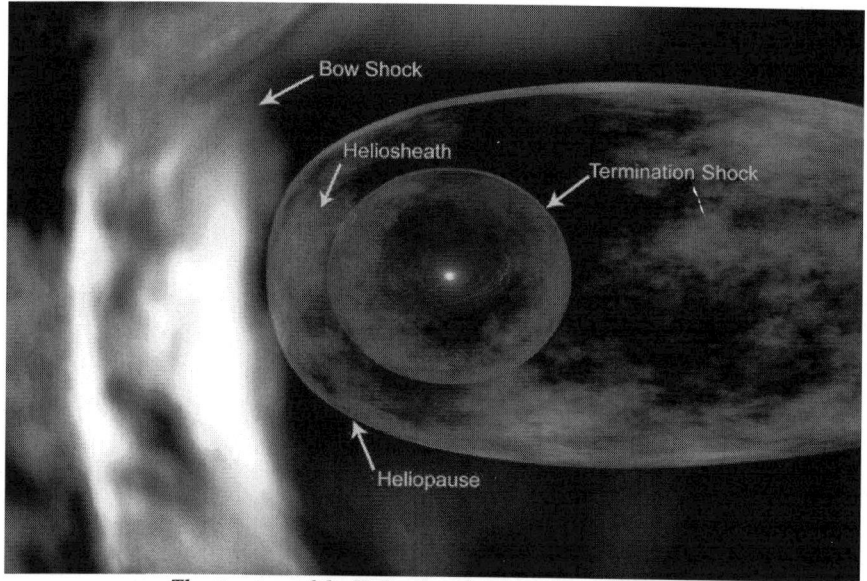

The structure of the Heliosphere (courtesy of Carl Murphy)

The Russian National Academy of Sciences in Novosibirsk, Siberia, have been carrying out little known research into the movement of the heliosphere through the galaxy. They have found that we are moving into an area of space where there is a higher energetic frequency. The Russians have observed glowing, excited plasma at the leading edge of the heliosphere (6). The plasma used to be only 10 astronomical units thick (an astronomical unit is the distance from the earth to the Sun, 93 million miles). This was given as the average thickness at the front of the heliosphere. It is now 100 astronomical units deep, which equates to a thousand percent increase in the thickness. But the front end of the heliosphere is also 1000 times *brighter* than before.

Our solar system appears to be moving into an area of space where the energy is more highly charged. This higher-charged energy excites the plasma that increases the brightness; this energy then flows into the Sun, which in turn emits the energy and spreads it out along the equatorial plane, which is called the ecliptic (the 'horizon' of the solar system). Wilcock believes this saturates interplanetary space, which then causes solar emissions to travel faster and charge up the energy of the planets, including all life on them too.

"And this is conscious energy that is changing how the planet works, how it functions, and what kind of life it supports. The harmonics of the DNA spiral itself are altering. That's the real, hidden cause of spontaneous mass evolutions in previous epochs of time. All this is happening all at the same time, and it's all working up to a crescendo where there is going to be a sudden shift" (7).

THE PHOTON BELT

In 1961, according to several by new age sources, Paul Otto Hesse discovered a 'photon belt' circling the central sun of the Pleiades, and, we are told, our solar system passes through it every 12,500 years, and will next be fully immersed in it in "2011-2012".

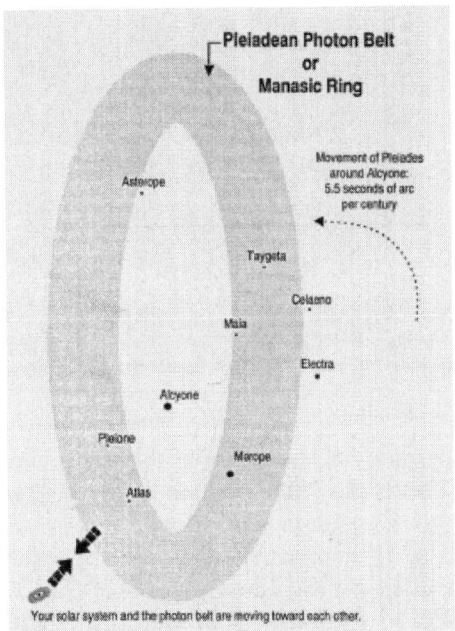

(Courtesy of Virginia Essene and Sheldon Nidle 1995)

The theory of the photon belt/band is seriously flawed and does not stand up under astronomical scrutiny. Geoff Stray, author of *Beyond 2012: Catastrophe or Ecstasy*, sums up the flaws (quoting from Cecil Adams) (8):

1) No photon belt or other such region of increased energy has been discovered. Photons in any case are merely particles of electromagnetic energy, which we commonly experience as light. Upon exposure to excess photons the most common transformation of your being is sunburn.
2) There's no "anomaly" near the Pleiades star cluster. The Pleiades are

surrounded by a nebula, or gas cloud. This cloud is composed not of photons but of dust and hydrogen gas.
3) The earth isn't heading toward the Pleiades but away from them. In the 1850s it was conjectured that the earth orbited the Pleiades, but this has long since been discredited.
4) Paul Otto Hesse is a German author of a book on Judgement Day and is unknown to astronomers.

This disinformation story actually begins in 1981 with an article on the "photon belt" written by Shirley Kemp and published in the Australian International UFO Research Society magazine, and reprinted in the February/March 1991 issue of Nexus magazine. Kemp's article focused on the Pleiades star cluster as the source of the photon belt and made no mention of the Galactic centre. The mixing of the photon belt concept with the idea of a Galactic centre came later, being injected by subsequent authors such as Robert Stanley and Barbara Hand Clow.

GALACTIC SUPERWAVE

Paul LaViolette proposes that the 'Photon Belt' covers up what is actually going on. He first came up with the 'Galactic Superwave' theory in 1983, where a regular pulsation at galactic centre creates a wave of cosmic rays that then fills the solar system with interstellar gas, occluding sunlight, and increasing solar flare activity. This may help explain the appearance of 'glowing plasma' at the front edge of our heliosphere, because we may be moving in to an area of the 'superwave'. In 1983 he proposed *"Galactic core explosions actually occur about every 13,000 - 26,000 years for major outbursts and more frequently for lesser events. The emitted cosmic rays escape from the core virtually unimpeded. As they travel radially outward through the galaxy, they form a spherical shell that advances at a velocity approaching the speed of light"* (9).

Not only do these time intervals correspond to the precession of the equinoxes, which have been recorded in ancient texts for millennia, but ice core samples also support his theory that huge amounts of interstellar dust stimulated solar activity 13,000 years ago. LaViolette confirms that at that time *"...the intensity and declination of the earth's magnetic field underwent major variations in step with the eleven-year sunspot cycle. The amplitude of these cycles was hundreds of times larger than modern geomagnetic solar cycles, suggesting that solar flare activity at that time was also hundreds of times more intense, approaching levels normally observed in T Tauri stars"* (10).

According to LaViolette, galactic centre is not a black hole, but rather a super-massive energy object that 'explodes' periodically, with 2012 being the next possible 'hit'.

GALACTIC ALIGNMENT

John Major Jenkins, author of *Galactic Alignment* and *Maya Cosmogenesis* has discovered evidence that the solstice sun is aligning with the galactic equator. Through several years of research and time spent with the Quiche Maya of Guatemala, he soon realised there was a distinct connection to the end date of the Mayan calendar and the process of our solar system aligning with Galactic centre (also incorrectly called the 'Central Sun' and 'Hunab Ku' by New-Agers). He also decoded the meaning behind the 13 baktun cycle. In his book *Maya Cosmogenesis 2012* , he describes how the final cycle of, 5,125 years is the fifth of a series of five eras together totalling about 26,000 – one cycle of the precession of the equinoxes. According to Jenkins, the Hindus, the ancient Nordic people, the Babylonians and the ancient Egyptians also knew about galactic alignment.

The 'bulge' in the centre of the Milky Way is the location of galactic centre. The galactic anti-centre is the area of the Pleiades and Gemini. But it is the Pleiades that have always been associated with higher consciousness. This might give some indication as to why the Maya were interested in the Pleiades, because it is the symbolic crown chakra of the galaxy! With the 'superwave' charging through the galaxy from galactic centre to anti-centre, metaphysically speaking this represents the kundalini energy rising up through the chakras, but on a slightly bigger scale. We are heading into the 'galactic kundalini', so we had better get ready!

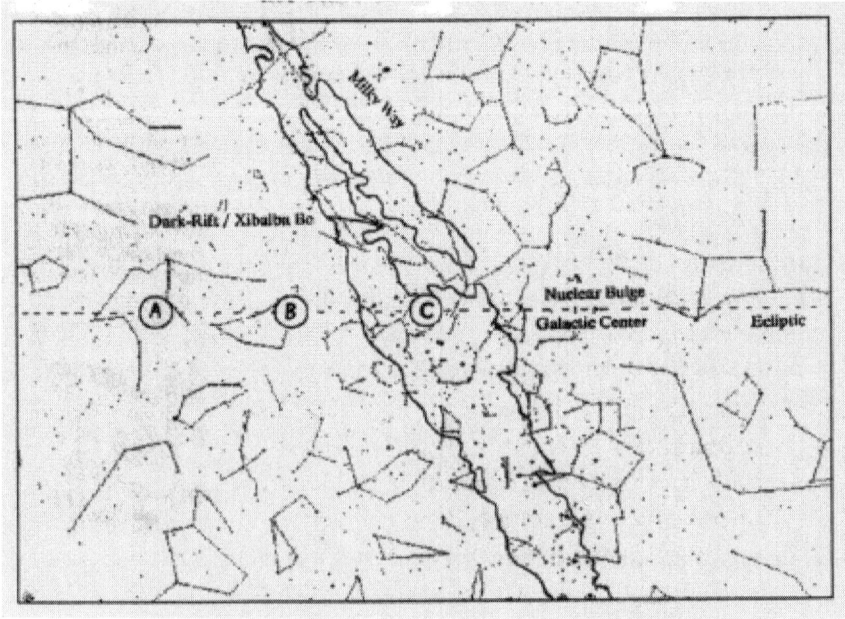

The convergence of the December solstice sun with Galactic Centre
A: 8000 years ago. B: 4000 years ago C: 2012 (from John Major Jenkins)

When we reach winter solstice 2012, earth's polar axis will be aligned towards the sun and galactic centre. The radiation coming through the ecliptic from the sun, and directly from galactic core could enter into the earth in a profound way. The Maya ended or 'turned over' their calendar at this point, suggesting they believed time as we know it was coming to an end (It will be the completion of the 13 baktun cycle, but not the end of their long count calendar, which 'turns over' and continues. Interestingly, there is a Mayan calendar date that is pinpointed to 21st October 4772AD!).

No one is quite sure what the effect will be, but as you may be aware there are plenty of theories. As the alignment happens, the earth will align with the plane of the galaxy and cause a "*field – effect energy reversal*", allowing us to resonate with the source of the field. According to John Major Jenkins, this will be the completion of the human spiritual embryogenesis, which is measured by the Mayan calendar, culminating in a "pole shift" in the collective psyche, and the birth of our Higher Selves. This last day of the Great Cycle, the Maya called the "Day of Creation" (11).

Wilcock believes it will be the point of "ascension", where our DNA becomes fully activated and we reach our ultimate potential. He suggests, in third dimensional reality, that there will be a mass extinction of our species, but believes that this is a cover for entering into a higher dimension. Willaru Huayta, a messenger for the Incas of Peru has told us that 2013 is the end of their calendar. Some Pueblo nation Americans say the 'Great purification' spoken of in the Hopi prophecy will be over by 2012. Maurice Cotterell and Adrian Gilbert believe the solar cycles will *all* reach 'solar maximum' on this date. Terence McKenna in *Time-Wave Zero*, found that the peak of 'novelty' will also be on December 21st 2012 (although originally on 17th December 2012).

Phylis Atwater (also known as P.M.H Atwater), author of numerous books about near-death experiences, has researched the NDE phenomenon in children. She found that many of the children were reporting earth changes that peaked around the year 2012 and concluded her research by declaring that this would be the "*final blossoming and fruition*" of the "*fifth root race*" (ibid). She went on to author two books specifically about the Indigo children, linking their development with the ending of the 13 Baktun cycle and how the "*fifth root race*" will lead us peacefully through the 2012 earth changes.

THE OCTAHEDRAL UNIVERSE

In a scientific paper discussing super-clusters, called *The Egg-Carton Universe* by Drs. E.Battaner and E.Florido, there is an image showing the shape of a local part of the cosmos. When I first saw this on Wilcock's ascension2000.com website, I could not believe this wasn't big news. This should rewrite cosmology in one go. Not only does this information collate into the idea that the entire Cosmos is shifting from an Octahedron to a Star-Tetrahedron geometry, but *it shows the lines of force connecting and travelling through galaxies.* With Paul LaViolette's theory of 'Galactic superwaves' and Dimitriev's suggestion of an 'area of highly charged space', this image demonstrates the idea that what our solar system is moving in to is in fact Universal energy.

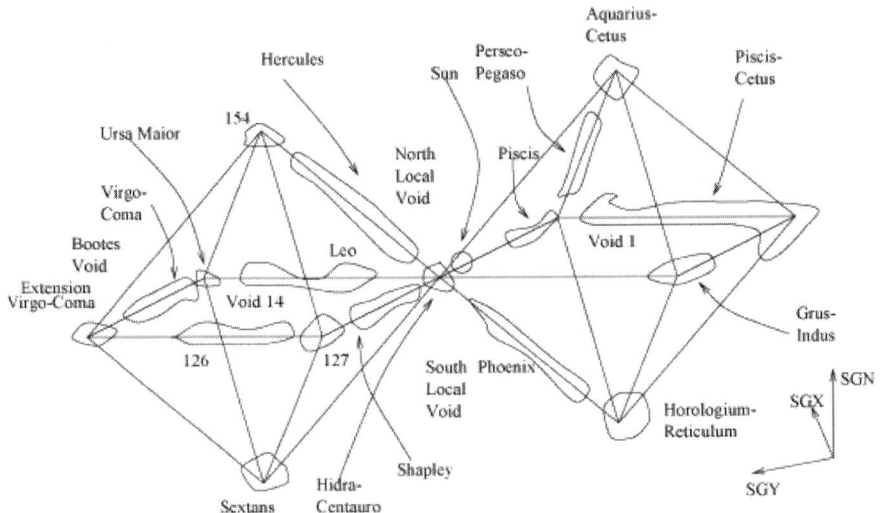

The two large octahedra closer to the Milky Way. (Battaner and Florido, 1997)

One can see within the diagram how the lines of force travel from one end of a galaxy to the other. In our galaxy, this would be galactic centre (between Sagittarius and Scorpio) and galactic anti-centre (Pleiades and Gemini). So are we going to all experience Universal energy? The lines of force are the geometric binder of the Universe, the divine shape of the entire cosmos. What we may have stumbled across here is the shape of God (or part of God). It also suggests the idea that we will experience our Creator. Perhaps this is what happens every 26,000 years.

Maurice Cotterell discovered that the sun also has the same inner octahedral geometric structure, as can be seen in this diagram (on next page). The sun has evenly-spaced points along the equator that emit regular showers of charged energy particles (6). Four times every month these negatively or positively charged particles reach the earth. The diagram shows how if the points are mapped out, they follow an octahedral geometry. (Note that these are not solar flares.)

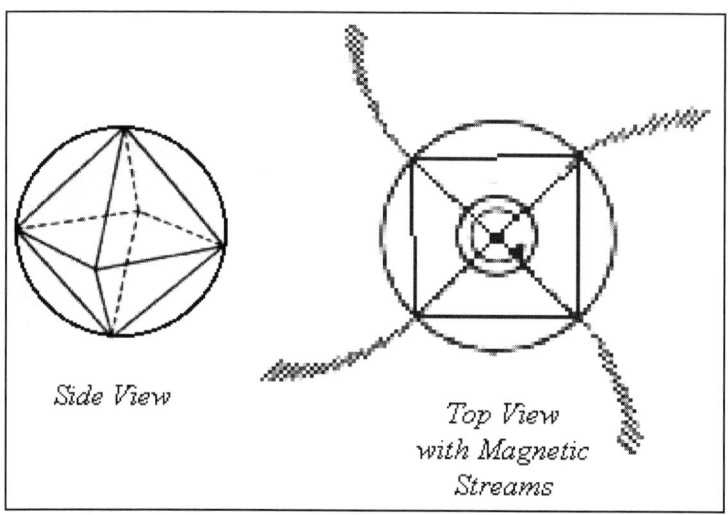

Octahedral energy patterns within the Sun (Wilcock 2000)

Does this then suggest that the human race are preparing for a dimensional shift? We have looked at some evidence implying that DNA mutation may be a key factor. The Chinese researchers have found that those people with activated DNA have these 'extra human functions'. It is also evident that the earth is going through this shift, with changes in the atmosphere, magnetic field and the energetic geometric structure. All the evidence points back to the Psychic children. Do they really hold the key?

6. BREATHING IN THE COSMOS

If we can imagine the Cosmos exhaling in a super-massive 'breathing' cycle; as described by Hindu mystics as 'The out-breath of Brahma'; we can begin to imagine that we are coming to the end of a billions-of-years-old out-breath of the Divine Being. As we enter this last stage of the cycle we can microcosmically reflect on our own breath, imagining that our last breath is imminent. When we are born, the first thing we do is breathe. When we die, the last thing we do is breathe. Our breath defines the start and the end of life as we know it and carries us safely through. Our own breathing cycle is a constant breathing in and out until it all ends. We then die.

If we were to take a closer look at the breath in slow motion, we would see that towards the end of the breath, it gradually slows down. Breathing in and out is not as clear-cut as it may seem. Also, after the slowing down of the breath, it does actually stop for a moment, before the next inhale. Is this what is happening with the Universe? Is there a slowing down followed by a pause? If so, how long is this pause and what are the effects?

This book has proposed that we are at the end of a great cycle, and that the Cosmos is showing signs that this is the case. It also suggests that this is affecting us as Humans in a profound and liberating way, and we are being stimulated to get ready for the coming change. As we all know, it appears that time is speeding up and it just keeps getting faster. If time/space were slowing down to standstill, would this suggest that there is less time in a day than we are used to? Although we still have our normal daily cycles of night and day with 24 hours, there is now less 'actual' time within that day. A friend of mine felt that there was only 16 hours in a full day now and not 24, although the clocks still read the same. We can simply not do as much as we once could in a single day, which can be very frustrating and stressful.

A new interpretation of time is needed. We can start by letting go of the clock and marking the times of day as 'midday', 'afternoon', 'dusk' etc (although this might be difficult for bus drivers!). We can then get back to the natural cycles of harmonic time. This is where the ancient Maya come in. Their view of time has been accepted as the most accurate on earth, stretching back thousands of years. They knew about the ending of the 'out breath' and pinpointed this date to December 21st 2012. They knew about the cycles of venus, the sun and even our galaxy – the Milky Way. They used various calendars to record different cycles through the ages – from a 260-day sacred cycle, through to the 26,000-year precessional cycle. But the best thing about the Maya is that all their calculations were incredibly accurate, even to today's standards.

Five cycles of 5,125 years come to an abrupt end on Winter Solstice 2012. Catastrophists believe this is the end of the world. Religions believe the 'pure' will go to Heaven. But modern seekers and freethinkers are beginning to see this in a completely different way. The Maya knew the current 13 baktun cycle would have finished by then. They knew time would come to a standstill. They knew we would enter the 'Now'. Is this the real reason the calendar ends on this particular date? Are we entering into 'non-time' where everything exists simultaneously in the Now? The 'Rapture' is potentially the shift into the present moment. 'The Great Purification' will be through, and we will be riding the hyper-dimensional wave of grace for eternity and a single moment – it's all the same in 'non-time'. No one knows exactly what this will feel like, but some of us are beginning get some clues.

There is a Universal purification taking place and we are obviously an integral part of the process. A re-balancing is occurring on every level, to get ready for the interval of 'non-time' before the in-breath of Brahma begins and time returns to our consciousness. Humans have been held back from reaching their full potential by being guided out of natural time - disconnecting from the cosmic harmonic synchronic order. The Gregorian calendar has done a good job with its unnatural ego-based count.

An overdue genetic leap is currently taking place that is helping humanity reach a critical mass of higher consciousness just in time for 'non-time'. To enter safely into such a high frequency after 2012, we have to re-tune our bodies to this higher vibration before we get there, otherwise we will short-circuit, panic and not be in the ready state to enter this realm of 'Now'. Is it any wonder that Buddhism and new-age techniques are on the increase? They are allowing us to get used to the 'Now' and to stay there in peace.

Getting back into time using the natural frequencies is also an opportunity to get free from any type of mind control. Time and mind rely on each other. In fact they are pretty much the same thing. Time cannot exist without mind. The mind is strengthened by time. The mind only *thinks* there is time because that is all it has been told since it can remember. One of the first things I remember was being taught how to read a clock. From this early age programming is easy. Reprogramming is time-consuming, but essential for freedom of the mind. The use of natural time is such a tool to release us from this disharmonic bondage. When we decide to re-program ourselves, we become in tune with the galactic frequency that has been blocked all of our lives by the Gregorian calendar. We are moving into the realm of the galaxy with potential to witness the Universe. We are becoming galactic beings. The research into the galaxy as explained in chapter six indicates that the Galaxy is aligning for the first time in 26,000 years, just as we start to look at her again. The Maya are helping us along this late path, but as we will soon see in 2012, it was all right on schedule.

Imagine the Aether as space and the movement of Aether as Time. The lines of force that bind the planetary grid and the geometry that hold it together combine to give the Earth Mother a strong aura, chakras and meridians. All these parts of the human are energetically represented on earth. It is also worth remembering that we are part of the earth in a profound way. The earth cannot exist without us and we cannot exist without the earth. We are all *the same*.

The bridging of awareness through studying the planetary grid brings one into planetary consciousness. A level of consciousness that not only spiritually develops us, but is now an essential act of survival. When we reach planetary consciousness, we start looking outwards from the surface of the earth, as though we are always looking at the stars and other galaxies, carrying our mother on our back. I'm sure if you looked hard enough, the true nature of the cosmos would reveal itself. As humans, we self-reflect with others around us, but the earth only reflects with the stars and other higher forms of consciousness, and galactic centre is literally on the horizon, waiting for us to return.

The reflection of the cosmos is echoed within our genetics. The alignment of the galaxy is synchronising with the alignment of our DNA. The sacred geometries that are mutating in the earth and the galaxy are also stimulating and resonating with the DNA of all life on earth. This is where the children come in. The youngest beings of Gaia are the first to show the signs of an overdue genetic leap and consciousness expansion.

From a human level, this new-breed is leading the way into a new paradigm. The purest, most humble and by far the most intelligent beings to grace this tiny planet; the Psychic children are the first to show the signs of this higher state of planetary and galactic consciousness. A new level of consciousness and intelligence is surpassing all expectations and gradually leading humanity into a new era of existence. Scientific studies are documenting these changes within the DNA and quantum physics is starting to give some answers regarding the nature of the Universe. Prophecies and prayers are being fulfilled as we enter into the 'Shift of the Ages'. These children are bringing a higher vibration to our planet. They are living evidence that humanity and the earth are beginning to "ascend" together. Establishing scientific evidence that this is the case has been quite a task, but to my constant surprise, there is stunning proof of this statement. Its not only the planet and humanity who are ascending, it's the entire Universe. God is shifting up a gear and we are going along for the ride whether we like it or not.

Impetus to change is prevalent in the minds of children, is beginning to spread through the planetary grid and affect more of us than ever before. Is it any wonder that the prime-directive of many of the children is to spread awareness of the importance of the planets energetic matrix and to urge us to get out on the land, tune in, and give the Mother a helping hand. Gaia is beginning to communicate to those who wish to listen, and the children are the ones hearing her initial call. As it said in the Bible, perhaps it's time to allow *"a child to lead them"*, as we prepare for the final call before the dimensional shift of 2012.

The children with the second sight
a natural thing so that they might
grow graceful, humble and when they do
the Golden Age will start anew.

APPENDIX :
Planetary Grid Points

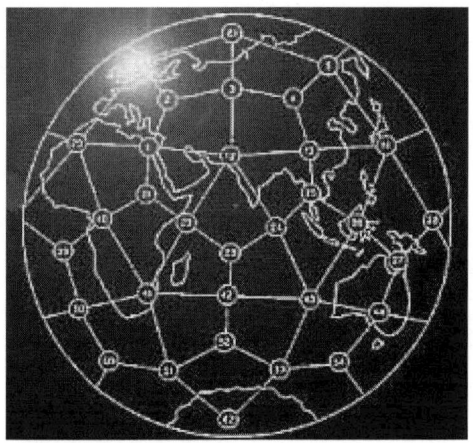

1. Great Pyramid at Giza, Egypt; r
2. Western Russia; unique soil composition1
3. Tyumen oil find
4. Lake Baikal, Northern Mongolia; unique soil composition1, 3/4 of the plants and animals (1000 species) are unique, megaliths
5. Sea of Okhotsk; major Soviet defense research site
6. Amchita Island, Aleutian Islands, Bering Sea
7. Gulf of Alaska, Exxon Valdez oil spill
8. Buffalo Lake, Alberta, Canada; major concentration of medicine wheels
9. Hudson Bay, north magnetic pole; Ugansk Bay, Eskimo art complex, Chubb meteor crater
10. Mid-atlantic underwater ridge to 37
11. Scotland; northern British Isles, Maes Howe, Ring of Brodger, Callenish megaliths; Loch Ness
12. Karachi, Pakistan; Indus Valley, ancient Mohenjo Daro culture; d, birds overwinter
13. Ancient Du Jiang irrigation system, natural home of the panda
14. Iwo Jima, southern Japan, seismic activity, Japan's Devils's Sea; d
15. Midway Island
16. Hawaiian islands; d
17. Hopi culture, Hohokom waterworks, Four Corners; r, wheel observed in Gemini photos
18. Bimini atoll, Bahamas; area of Bermuda triangle; wheel observed in Gemini photos, d
19. Atlantis Fracture
20. Morocco, Algerian megalithic ruins, Ahaggar ancient cave art; w, d, fault line to Pakistan, #12; birds overwinter
21. Zimbabwe, Africa; Sudan, ancient Kush, contemporary locust plague, near Khartoum, ecliptic crosses here and #31
22. Somalia Basin, equator
23. Chagos archipelago
24. Equator
25. Bangkok, Angkor Wat

26. Sarawak, Solomon Islands, Borneo megaliths, equator, center of spice trade, Toraja
27. Gulf of Carpentaria, massive gold reserves
28. Ponapé, Solomon Islands, equator
29. Marshall Islands
30. Phoenix Islands; Nova Canton trough; equator
31. Society Island; Caroline Islands, ecliptic crosses here
32. Mid south Pacific; equator
33. Clipperton Islands
34. Galapagos Islands; junction of Cocos and Carnegie ridges; equator
35. Lima, Peru; Lake Punrrun in coastal highlands; boundary of Nazca plate, stones of ice, seat of ancient Peru
36. Amazonian ruins, Yanomomo homelands; equator
37. Guiana Basin, Vema Fracture
38. Romanche Fracture; equator
39. Ascension Island
40. Gabon, west Africa; spontaneous U-235 atomic explosion 1 million years ago; equator
41. L'uyengo on the Usutu River in Swaziland, Great Zimbabwe, site of earliest pre-humans; d, r, birds overwinter
42. Intersection of Mid-Indian and Southwest Indian Ridges
43. Wharton Basin d
44. South Australia aboriginal land; Marilinga atomic test site, Wilpena Pound huge meteor impact site
45. Peruvian megaliths, UFO sightings; d
46. Undifferentiated south pacific ocean
47. Easter Island megaliths; d
48. Argentine Tafi megaliths
49. Rio de Janeiro; d
50. Atlantic Ridge
51. Enderby Abyssal Plain
52. Kerguelen Plateau
53. South Indian Basin
54. Kangaroo Fracture
55. Emerald Basin
56. Udintsev Fracture
57. Eltanin Fracture
58. South American tip, edge of the Haeckel Deep
59. East Scotia Basin Earth
60. South Atlantic Ridge
61. North Pole
62. South Pole

Notes:
1. Christopher Bird
r= radiation
d= diamond center

References

Chapter 1 – The Children
1. J.Henry & M.Day. The Sunday Telegraph *11.4.04*
2. Published in *Nexus Magazine*, Volume 2, # 24 February-March 1995.

Chapter 2 – The Hawaii Conference
1. http://www.earthstarcreations.com/grandmother_chandra.htm
2. http//:www.emissaryoflight.com
3. Hoagland, Richard. *The Monuments of Mars: City on the Edge of Forever*
4. Stray, Geoff. *Diagnosis2012.co.uk.*
5. from *Vanished: Strange Cases of Unsolved Disappearances* by Stephen Wagner
6. Dunford, Barry. The Holy Land of Scotland: Jesus in Scotland & the Gospel of the Grail. P.130

Chapter 3 – The Planetary Grid
1. Cathie, Bruce L. *The Energy Grid: Harmonic 695 – The Pulse of the Universe.*1997
2. Joan Oceans personal account - http://www.etfriends.com/LFAS.html
3. Kay, Jane. *San Fransisco Chronicle* - July 16th 2002
4. Childress, David Hatcher. *Anti-Gravity and the World Grid.*
5. Munck, Carl. The Code - *Video Series*
6. Wilcock, David. *Shift of The Ages.* Chapter 11
7. Ibid
8. Flem-Ath, Rand & Wilson, Colin. *The Atlantis Blueprint.* P.66
9. reprinted in *Anti-Gravity and the World Grid.* Originally in the Russian science Journal 'Khimiyai Zhizn' or 'Chemistry of Life'
10. William Becker & Bethe Hagens. *The Planetary Grid: A New Synthesis.* From Pursuit Magazine vol.17, no.2 1984
11. This is a long story that will be fully documented in the forthcoming book *The Glastonbury Grail* by David Hatfield.
12. Wilcock, David. *Shift of the Ages.* Ch.11

Chapter 4 – Nutrition for the New Human
1. J.Henry & M.Day. The Sunday Telegraph *11.4.04*
2. Rappoport, Jon. *School Violence – The Psychiatric Drugs Connection* in Nexus vol.6, no.5 August/September 1999.
3. ABC News, USA. 17th Feb 2000.
4. JAMA 284[4],26.7.2000. jama.ama-asan.org/issues/
5. Virtue, Doreen. *The Care and Feeding of Indigo Children.*
6. Blythman, Joanna. *The Daily Mail .* 26 May 2004.
7. *Chemical World* Part 2. P.23. 'The Guardian' supplement. May 2004.
8. Ibid. P.22.
9. Erasmus, Udo. *Fats that Heal, Fats that Kill* booklet. P.5.
10..Blaylock, Russell L MD. *Medical Sentinel* vol 4, no.6, nov-dec 1999
11. Ikonomidou, C and Turski,L, "*Glutamate in Neurodegenerative Disorders*" in Stone, T.W.(ed.), CNS Neurotransmitters and Neuromodulators:Glutamate. 1995 pp253-272.
12. Department of Health and Human Services, *Report on All Adverse Reactions in the Adverse Reaction Monitoring System,* February 25 and 28, 1994.
13. Compiled by researchers, physicians, and artificial sweetener experts for *Mission Possible*, a group dedicated to warning consumers about aspartame.
14. Russell L.Blaylock MD. *Medical Sentinel* vol 4, no.6, nov-dec 1999.
15. William duffy. *The Sweetest Poison of All.* Extracted from Nexus Magazine, Volume 7, Number 1. December 1999 - January 2000.
16. Doreen Virtue. *The Care and Feeding of Indigo Children.* PP155-156

17. ibid.
18. Cott, Allan, *Orthomolecular Approach to the Treatment of Learning Disabilities*, synopsis of reprint article issued by the Huxley Institute for Biosocial Research, New York.
19. ADA Courier, January 1993, Volume 32, Number 1. (26) "FDA Rejects AHPA Stevia Petition" by Mark Blumenthal, Whole Foods, April 1994.
20. Sellman, Sherrill. *Xylitol: Our sweet salvation?* In Nexus vol 10, No 1. Dec 2002 – Jan 2003.
21. *Chemical World*. Part 2. P.6.
22. Pitchford, Paul. *Healing with Whole Foods: Oriental traditions and Modern Medicine.* P.259.
23. *Chemical World*. Part 2. P.24.
24. Vaughan, Liz *Stop Fluoridation Campaign moves into Gear* from 'Namaste' magazine Vol.6, issue 4, 2003.
25. *journal of the American Dental Association* Vol.XXIII P.74.
26. *In Harm's Way: Toxic Threats to Child Development* A Report by Greater Boston Physicians for Social Responsibility May 2000.
27. Sample, Ian and Kinnes, Sally. *Chemistry Lesson* in Chemical World P.10.
28. Atkins, Lucy. *What's in Baby Products?* in 'Chemical World'. The Guardian 8th May 2004.
29. Sample, Ian and Kinnes, Sally. *Chemistry Lesson* in Chemical World P.10
30. Sample, Ian *When You're Pregnant.* Chemical World P.23
31. Fraser, Lorraine *The Mail on Sunday* 9th April 2000
32. *How To Raise a Healthy Child.....in Spite of Your Doctor,* by Robert Mendelsohn MD
33. Coulter, Harris, *Vaccination, Social Violence and Criminality: The Medical assault on the American Brain.* The Centre for Empirical Medicine, Washington DC 1990
34. McTaggart, Lynne. *What Doctors Don't Tell You.* P.117
35. Hickman, Maureen. *Shaken Baby Syndrome or Adverse Vaccine Reaction?* In Nexus Vol.7, No.6. October-November 2000
36. *Chemical World.* Part 2, P.32.
37. *The Daily Mail.* April 11 2004.
38. Pitchford P.650
39. Pitchford P.254
40. Virtue, Doreen *The Care and Feeding of Indigo Children* P.153
41. Phytate reduction of zinc absorption has been demonstrated in numerous studies. These results are summarised in Leviton, Richard, *Tofu, Tempeh, Miso and Other Soyfoods: The 'Food of the Future' - How to Enjoy Its Spectacular Health Benefits,* Keats Publishing, Inc., New Canaan, CT, USA, 1982, p. 1415.
42. Holford, Patrick *The Optimum Nutrition Bible* P.316.
43. Virtue P.154.
44. Adam, Sean. *Etherium Gold Improves Brain Balance and Learning Ability By Stimulating Electro-chemical Reactions in the Brain,* 'The Alpha Learning Institute, Switzerland. Nov 5th 2002. www.alphalearning.com.
45. Dallas, Robert E, Ph.D. *A Preliminary Inquiry into the Biological and Neurophysiological Effects of Etherium Gold.* The Mind Spa. June 2nd 1998.
46. *The Child Scrambler: What a Mobile Can do to a Youngster's Brain in Two minutes* in The Sunday Mirror December 27th 2001.
47. Maisch, Don. *Children and Mobile Phone Use* in Nexus Vol 9, No 4 June/July 2002.
48. *Mobile & Cordless Phones:Microwave Madness* Leaflet. Summer 2003.

Chapter 5 – DNA Activation
1. Braden, Gregg. *Walking Between the Worlds: The science of compassion p.80*
2. *Vernetzte Intelligenz* by Grazyna Fosar and Franz Bludorf (summarised and translated by Baerbel):See fosar-bludorf.com for translated articles.

3. From a review of a Gregg Braden workshop in Monterey, California. Robert E. Detzler.
4. *The Ancient Secret of the Flower of Life* Volume II. Drunvalo Melchizedek.P.449
5. *Prophecy, Prayer & Choice*. Gregg Braden Interviewed by Miriam Knight
New Connexion - Portland, Oregon. January/February 2000
6. *The Ancient Secret of the Flower of Life* Volume II. Drunvalo Melchizedek. P.445-446.
7. *The Times*. 2nd November 1997
8. Gardner, Laurence. *Lost Secrets of the Sacred Ark.*
9. http://www.whitepowdergold.com
10. For the most comprehensive and regularly updated information in this regard, see Barry Carter's ORMUS site at: http://www.subtleenergies.com/ormus/whatisit.htm
11. Gardner, Laurence. *Lost Secrets of the Sacred Ark.*.P.182
12. "Electric Genes" in *Scientific American.* David Patterson. May 1995. P.33-34. Note that superconductivity does not need physical contact.
13. Vipassana is taught at centres throughout the world. www.dhamma.org.
14. harmonicinnerprizes.com/alphalearning_institute.html in a letter by Sean Adam, research director to the producers of Etherium gold, Harmonic Innerprizes.
15. Gardner, Laurence. *Lost Secrets of the Sacred Ark.*. P.122-123.
16. Utiger, Robert D., "Melatonin, the Hormone of Darkness", in the *New England Journal of Medicine,* vol 327, no.19, Nov 1992.
17. www.heartmath.org/ResearchPapers/DNAPhantom/DNAPhantom.html.
18. Narby, Jeremy. *The Cosmic Serpent: DNA & the Origins of Knowledge.*
19. *The Ancient Secret of the Flower of Life* Volume I. Drunvalo Melchizedek. P.193

Chapter 6 – Galactic Alignment 2012
1. Wilcock, David, Maurice Cotterell and the Great Sunspot Cycle in 'Shift of the Ages', ascension2000.com
2. Lockwood, Mike. (230% increase in solar magnetic field since 1901) (1998) ascension2000.com/solarmag.html.
3. Wilcock, David. *The Transformation of the Solar System* Ch.8. 'The Divine Cosmos'. Ascension2000.com
4. Pasichnyk, Richard. The Vital Vastness – Volume Two: The Living Cosmos. (2002) http://www.livingcosmos.com
5. Wilcock, David. Ch.1. 'The Divine Cosmos'. Ascension2000.com.
6. Wilcock, David. The Matrix is a Reality. 10th April 2003. Ascension2000.com
7. Wilcock, David .The Scientific Blueprint for Ascension. 2001
8. Stray, Geoff. http://www.diagnosis2012.co.uk
9. *Beyond 2012* p.91 note 10. Originally from Violette. Paul la , *Earth Under Fire* p.187
10. *Beyond 2012* p.91. Originally from Violette. Paul la , *Earth Under Fire* p.187
11. Jenkins, John Major. *Maya Cosmogenesis* 2012. p.330

Websites:
www.psychicchildren.co.uk - Hugh's Indigo child portal
www.newhuman.co.uk - Nutrition for the new human
www.childrenofthenewearth.com - Regular Indigo magazine
www.avalonrising.co.uk - Glastonbury earth mysteries
www.emissaryoflight.com - James Twyman's website.
www.spiritofmaat.com - Articles by Drunvalo Melchizedek & esoteric info.
www.SOULutions.co.uk- Indigo Child education.
www.grandmachandra.com - Chandra's website.
www.indigochild.com - Lee Carrol & Jan Tober's site.
www.joanocean.com - Dolphins and Whales
www.drboylan.com - ET encounters/Star chid article
www.divinecosmos.com - David Wilcock
www.diagnosis2012.co.uk - Geoff Stray's 2012 super-site